PAUL SCHRADER: COLLECTED SCREENPLAYS I

by the same author

SCHRADER ON SCHRADER, AND OTHER WRITINGS
(edited by Kevin Jackson)
BRINGING OUT THE DEAD

PAUL SCHRADER
Collected Screenplays

VOLUME I
Taxi Driver
American Gigolo
Light Sleeper

faber and faber

This collection first published in 2002
by Faber and Faber Limited
3 Queen Square London WC1N 3AU

Typeset by Faber and Faber Ltd
Printed in England by Bookmarque Ltd, Croydon

A CIP record for this book
is available from the British Library
ISBN 0-571-21022-8

2 4 6 8 10 9 7 5 3 1

CONTENTS

Paul Schrader (right) confers with Richard Gere on location for *American Gigolo*.

INTRODUCTION

I have been drawn to a certain character: a person, usually male, who drifts on the edge of urban society, always peeping, looking into the lives of others. He'd like to have a life of his own but doesn't know how to get one.

I have written about him when he was in his twenties, angry, and a taxi driver; when he was in his thirties, narcissistic, and a gigolo; and when he was in his forties, anxious, and a drug dealer. I've written yet another script about him, now in his fifties, which I'd like to make after the film I'm currently preparing. Then I'll retire him. It's getting too difficult to finance existential character studies.

He's manifest in these screenplays but also present, to varying degrees, in other scripts of mine: *The Last Temptation of Christ*, *Mishima*, *Bringing Out the Dead*, and *Affliction*.

Looking back, it's not hard to see why I was drawn to him. I was raised in the bosom of the Christian Reformed Church, a Dutch Calvinist denomination. After graduation from Calvin College, I attended UCLA film school. Like many of my generation, I'd heard the siren song of rebellion and illicit behavior. For me, however, illicit behavior was as simple as seeing movies: they had been forbidden by family edict and synodical decree.

In Los Angeles I was not unlike Travis Bickle: a bundle of tightly wrapped contradictions, driving around, trying but unable to belong. Perhaps this is why, having 'liberated' myself, I revered the most rigid of artists (Bresson) and cultures (Japan). It's not unusual for a recently escaped convict to flee to a prison of another sort.

Taxi Driver was written in a chapter format because I wanted to capture the seeming randomness of Travis's life: he goes here, he does that, etc. *American Gigolo* was written in conventional script format because I was 'in' Hollywood, had sold scripts, and wanted scripts that looked like everyone else's.

With *Light Sleeper*, now an independent film-maker, I returned to the chapter format.

Plot is tricky in character studies. Ideally they should be plotless, dwelling on the complexities and contradictions of human behavior, guiding the viewer to one of several conclusions. That's unrealistic in the commercial cinema. The trick is to have just enough plot so that it seems like something is happening, but not so much that the viewer thinks it's about plot. *Taxi Driver* is circular. At the end of the narrative Travis has not been changed, he's been revealed.

At the end of *American Gigolo* I wanted to perversely plunge my lizardy protagonist into icy Bressonian waters, so I lifted the ending of *Pickpocket* and gave it to Julian Kay. A grace note as unwarranted as Christ's promise to the thief on the cross. When writing *Light Sleeper*, I felt that I should have used that ending there, not in *Gigolo*. So I stole again, this time from Bresson and myself, and reused the ending. For the next one I've got something else in mind.

Paul Schrader
October 2001

Taxi Driver

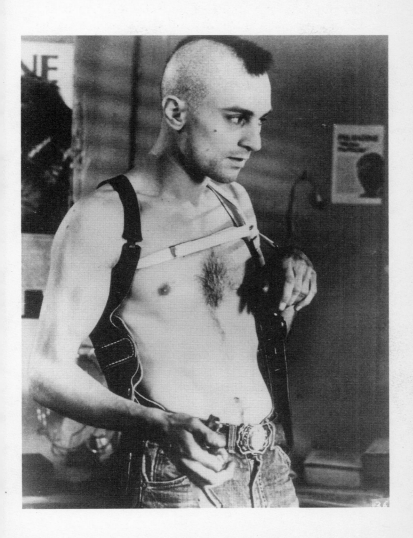

CAST AND CREW

MAIN CAST

TRAVIS BICKLE	Robert De Niro
IRIS	Jodie Foster
BETSY	Cybill Shepherd
SPORT	Harvey Keitel
ANDY, THE GUN SALESMAN	Steven Prince
TOM	Albert Brooks
WIZARD	Peter Boyle
CHARLES PALANTINE	Leonard Harris

MAIN CREW

Directed by	Martin Scorsese
Written by	Paul Schrader
Produced by	Michael Phillips
	Julia Phillips
Cinematography by	Michael Chapman
Edited by	Marcia Lucas
	Tom Rolf
	Melvin Shapiro
Music by	Bernard Hermann
Visual Consultant	David Nichols

'The whole conviction of my life now rests upon the belief that loneliness, far from being a rare and curious phenomenon, is the central and inevitable fact of human existence.'

Thomas Wolfe,
God's Lonely Man

Travis Bickle, aged twenty-six, lean, hard, the consummate loner. On the surface he appears good-looking, even handsome; he has a quiet steady look and a disarming smile which flashes from nowhere, lighting up his whole face. But behind that smile, around his dark eyes, in his gaunt cheeks, one can see the ominous strains caused by a life of private fear, emptiness, and loneliness. He seems to have wandered in from a land where it is always cold, a country where the inhabitants seldom speak. The head moves, the expression changes, but the eyes remain ever-fixed, unblinking, piercing empty space.

Travis is now drifting in and out of the New York City night life, a dark shadow among darker shadows. Not noticed, with no reason to be noticed, Travis is one with his surroundings. He wears rider jeans, cowboy boots, a plaid western shirt, and a worn beige Army jacket with a patch reading 'King Kong Company, 1968–70.'

He has the smell of sex about him: sick sex, repressed sex, lonely sex, but sex none the less. He is a raw male force, driving forward; toward what, one cannot tell. Then one looks closer and sees the inevitable. The clock spring cannot be wound continually tighter. As the earth moves toward the sun, Travis Bickle moves toward violence.

TRAVIS GETS A JOB

Film opens on exterior of Manhattan cab garage. Weather-beaten sign above driveway reads: 'Taxi Enter Here.' Yellow cabs scuttle in and out. It is winter, snow is piled on the curbs, the wind is howling.

Inside the garage are parked row upon row of multi-colored taxis. Echoing sounds of cabs idling, cabbies talking. Steamy breath and exhaust fill the air.

Corridor of cab company offices. Lettering on ajar door reads:

PERSONNEL OFFICE
Mavis Cab Company
Blue and White Cab Co.
Acme Taxi
Dependable Taxi Services
JRB Cab Company
Speedo Taxi Service

Sounds of office busy at work: shuffling, typing, arguing.

Personnel office is a cluttered disarray. Sheets with headings 'Mavis, B&W, Acme' and so forth are tacked to crumbling plaster wall. It is March. Desk is cluttered with forms, reports, and an old upright Royal typewriter.

Disheveled middle-aged New Yorker looks up from the desk. We cut in to ongoing conversation between the middle-aged personnel officer and a young man standing in front of his desk.

The young man is Travis Bickle. He wears his jeans, boots, and Army jacket. He takes a drag of his unfiltered cigarette.

The personnel officer is exhausted: he arrives at work exhausted. Travis is something else again. His intense steely gaze is enough to jar even the personnel officer out of his workaday boredom.

PERSONNEL OFFICER (O.S.)
No trouble with the Hack Bureau?

TRAVIS (O.S.)
No, sir.

PERSONNEL OFFICER (O.S.)
Got your license?

TRAVIS (O.S.)
Yes.

PERSONNEL OFFICER
So why do you want to be a taxi driver?

TRAVIS
I can't sleep nights.

PERSONNEL OFFICER
There's porno theaters for that.

TRAVIS
I know. I tried that.

The personnel officer, though officious, is mildly probing and curious. Travis is a cipher, cold and distant. He speaks as if his mind doesn't know what his mouth is saying.

PERSONNEL OFFICER
So what'ja do now?

TRAVIS
I ride around nights mostly. Subways, buses. See things. Figured I might as well get paid for it.

PERSONNEL OFFICER
We don't need any misfits around here, son.

A thin smile cracks almost indiscernibly across Travis's lips.

TRAVIS
You kiddin'? Who else would hack through South Bronx or Harlem at night?

PERSONNEL OFFICER
You want to work uptown nights?

TRAVIS
I'll work anywhere, any time. I know I can't be choosy.

PERSONNEL OFFICER
(*thinks a moment*)
How's your driving record?

TRAVIS
Clean. Real clean.
(*pause, thin smile*)
As clean as my conscience.

PERSONNEL OFFICER
Listen, son, you gonna get smart, you can leave right now.

                              TRAVIS
                           (*apologetic*)
Sorry, sir. I didn't mean that.

                    PERSONNEL OFFICER
Physical? Criminal?

                              TRAVIS
Also clean.

                    PERSONNEL OFFICER
Age?

                              TRAVIS
Twenty-six.

                    PERSONNEL OFFICER
Education?

                              TRAVIS
Some. Here and there.

                    PERSONNEL OFFICER
Military record?

                              TRAVIS
Honorable discharge. May, 1971.

                    PERSONNEL OFFICER
You moonlightin'?

                              TRAVIS
No, I want long shifts.

                    PERSONNEL OFFICER
                    (*casually, almost to himself*)
We hire a lot of moonlighters here.

                              TRAVIS
So I hear.

                    PERSONNEL OFFICER
                    (*looks up at Travis*)
Hell, we ain't that much fussy anyway. There's always

openings on one fleet or another.
> (*rummages through his drawer, collecting various pink,*
> *yellow, and white forms*)

Fill out these forms and give them to the girl at the desk, and leave your phone number. You got a phone?

TRAVIS

No.

PERSONNEL OFFICER

Well, then, check back tomorrow.

TRAVIS

Yes, sir.

Credits appear over scenes from Manhattan nightlife. The snow has melted; it is spring.

A rainy, slick, wet, miserable night in Manhattan's theater district. Cabs and umbrellas are congested everywhere; well-dressed pedestrians are pushing, running, waving down taxis. The high-class theater patrons crowding out of the midtown shows are shocked to find that the same rain that falls on the poor and common is also falling on them.

The unremitting sounds of honking and shouting play against the dull pitter-patter of rain. The glare of yellow, red, and green lights reflects off the pavements and autos.

'When it rains, the boss of the City is the taxi driver' – so goes the cabbies' maxim, proved true by this particular night's activity. Only the taxis seem to rise above the situation: they glide effortlessly through the rain and traffic, picking up whom they choose, spurning whom they choose, going where they please.

Further uptown, the crowds are neither so frantic nor so glittering. The rain also falls on the street bums and the aged poor. Junkies still stand around on rainy street corners, hookers still prowl rainy sidewalks. And the taxis service them too. All through the credits the exterior sounds are muted, as if coming from a distant room or storefront round the corner. The listener is at a safe but privileged distance.

After examining various strata of Manhattan nightlife, the camera begins to close in on one particular taxi, and it is assumed that this taxi is being driven by Travis Bickle.

The credits end.

WE MEET TRAVIS

Travis's yellow taxi pulls up in the foreground. On left rear door are lettered the words 'Dependable Taxi Service.'

We are somewhere in the upper fifties on Fifth Avenue. The rain has not let up.

An elderly woman climbs in the right rear door, crushing her umbrella. Travis waits a moment, then pulls away from the curb with a start.

Later, we see Travis's taxi: speeding down the rain-slicked avenue. The action is periodically accompanied by Travis's narration. He is reading from a haphazard personal diary.

> TRAVIS (V.O.)
> (*monotone*)
> April 10, 1972. Thank God for the rain which has helped wash the garbage and trash off the sidewalks.

Travis's point of view, of sleazy midtown side street: bums, hookers, junkies.

> I'm working a single now, which means stretch-shifts, six to six, sometimes six to eight in the a.m., six days a week.

A man in business suit hails Travis to the curb.

> It's a hustle, but it keeps me busy. I can take in three to three-fifty a week, more with skims.

Man in business suit, now seated in back seat, speaks up.

> MAN IN BUSINESS SUIT
> (*urgent*)
> Is Kennedy operating, cabbie? Is it grounded?

On the seat next to Travis is a half-eaten cheeseburger and order of french fries. He puts his cigarette down and gulps as he answers.

> TRAVIS
Why should it be grounded?

> MAN IN BUSINESS SUIT
Listen – I mean I just saw the needle of the Empire State Building. You can't see it for the fog!

> TRAVIS
Then it's a good guess it's grounded.

> MAN IN BUSINESS SUIT
The Empire State in fog means something, don't it? Do you know or don't you? What is your number, cabbie?

> TRAVIS
Have you tried the telephone?

> MAN IN BUSINESS SUIT
> *(hostile, impatient)*
There isn't time for that. In other words, you don't know.

> TRAVIS
No.

> MAN IN BUSINESS SUIT
Well, you should know, damn it, or who else would know? Pull over right here.
> *(points out of window)*
Why don't you stick your goddamn head out of the god-damn window once in a while and find out about the god-damn fog!

Travis pulls to the curb. The man in business suit stuffs a dollar bill into the pay drawer and jumps out of the cab. He turns to hail another taxi.

> Taxi! Taxi!

Travis writes up his trip card and drives away.

It is later that night. The rain has turned to drizzle. Travis drives through another section of Manhattan.

TRAVIS (V.O.)

I work the whole city, up, down, don't make no difference to me – does to some.

Streetside: Travis's point of view. Black prostitute wearing white vinyl boots, leopard-skin mini-skirt and blonde wig, hails taxi. On her arm hangs half-drunk seedy executive type.

Travis pulls over.

Prostitute and John (the executive type) climb into back seat. Travis checks out the action in rear-view mirror.

Some won't take spooks – Hell, don't make no difference to me.

Travis's taxi drives through Central Park. Grunts, groans coming from back seat. Prostitute and John going at it in back seat. He's having a hard time and she's probably trying to get him to come off manually.

JOHN (O.S.)

Oh, baby, baby.

PROSTITUTE (O.S.)
(*forceful*)

Come on.

Travis stares blankly ahead.

Travis's apartment. Camera pans silently across the interior, indicating this is not a new scene.

Travis is sitting at plain table, writing. He wears shirt, jeans, boots. An unfiltered cigarette rests in a bent coffee-can ashtray.

Close-up of notebook. It is a plain lined dimestore notebook and the words Travis is writing with a stubby pencil are those he is saying. The columns are straight, disciplined. Some of the writing is in pencil, some in ink. The handwriting is jagged. Camera continues to

*pan, examining Travis's apartment. It is unusual, to say the least. A
ratty old mattress is thrown against one wall. The floor is littered
with old newspapers, worn and unfolded street maps, and pornography. The pornography is of the sort that looks cheap but costs $10 a
throw – black-and-white photos of naked women tied and gagged
with black leather straps and clotheslines. There is no furniture other
than the rickety chair and table. A beat-up portable TV rests on an
upright melon-crate. The red silk mass in another corner looks like a
Vietnamese flag. Indecipherable words, figures, numbers are scribbled
on the plain plaster walls. Ragged black wires dangle from the wall
where the telephone once hung.*

> TRAVIS (V.O.)
>
> They're all animals anyway. All the animals come out at
> night: whores, skunk pussies, buggers, queens, fairies,
> dopers, junkies, sick, venal.
>
> (*a pause*)
>
> Someday a *real* rain will come and wash all this scum off
> the streets.

*Early morning, 6 a.m. The air is clean and fresh and the streets
nearly deserted.*

Exterior of taxi garage. Travis's taxi pulls into the driveway.

> Each night when I return the cab to the garage I have to
> clean the come off the back seat. Some nights I clean off
> the blood.

*Travis pulls his taxi into taxi garage stall. He reaches across the cab
and extracts a small vial of Bennies from the glove compartment.*

*He stands next to the cab, straightens his back, and tucks the bottle
of pills into his jacket pocket. He lowers his head, looks into back
seat, opens rear door, and bends inside. He shakes a cigarette out of
his pack of Camels and lights it.*

*Slight timecut. Travis books in at garage office. Old, rotting slabs of
wood are screwed to a gray crumbling concrete wall. Each available
space is covered with hand-lettered signs, time schedules, check-out
sheets, memos. The signs read:*

BE ALERT!
THE SANE DRIVER
IS ALWAYS READY
FOR THE UNEXPECTED

ALL NIGHT DRIVERS
HAVING PERSONAL INJURY
ACCIDENTS
MUST PHONE IN AT ONCE TO
JUDSON 2–3410
AND MUST FILE A REPORT *PROMPTLY*
AT 9 AM THE FOLLOWING MORNING AT
43 W. 61ST.

SLOW DOWN
AND GAUGE SPEED TO
ROAD CONDITIONS
YOU CAN'T STOP
ON A DIME!

A half-dozen haggard cabbies hang around the office. Their shirts are wrinkled, their heads dropping, their mouths incessantly chattering. We pick up snatches of cabbie small talk.

FIRST CABBIE

. . . hadda piss like a bull steer, so I pull over on 10th Ave., yank up the hood, and do the engine job.
    (gestures as if taking a piss into the hood)
There I am with my dong in my hand when a guy come up and asks if I need any help. 'Just checking the battery,' I says, and, meanwhile . . .

Takes imaginary piss.

SECOND CABBIE

If he thinks I'm going up into The Jungle this time of night, he can shove it.

THIRD CABBIE
(talking into pay-phone)
Fuck that Violets First. Fucking saddle horse. No, no, the

OTB. Fuck them. No, it was TKR. TCR and I'da made
seven fucking grand. Fuck them too. All right, what about
the second race?

FOURTH CABBIE

Over at Love, this hooker took on the whole garage. Blew
the whole fucking joint and they wouldn't even let her use
the drinking fountain.

*Travis hands his trip sheet to the cab official, nods slightly, turns,
and walks toward the door.*

*Outside, Travis walks pleasantly down Broadway, his hands in his
jacket pockets. The sidewalks are deserted, except for diligent fruit
and vegetable vendors setting up their stalls. He takes a deep breath
of fresh air, pulls a white pill from his pocket, pops it into his mouth.*

*He turns a corner, keeps walking. Ahead of him is a twenty-four-
hour porno theater. The theater, a blaze of cheap Day-Glo reds and
yellows, is an offense to the clear, crisp morning air. The permanent
lettering reads, 'Adam Theater. 16 mm Sound Features.' Underneath, today's features are hand-lettered: 'Six-Day Cruise' and
'Beaver Dam.' Travis stops at the box-office, purchases a ticket, and
walks in.*

Porno theater.

*Inside the porno theater, Travis stands in the aisle for a moment. He
turns round, walking back toward the concession stand.*

*A plain, dumpy-looking girl sits listlessly on a stool behind the
shabby concession stand. A plaster-of-paris Venus de Milo sits atop a
piece of purple velvet cloth on the counter. The sound of the feature
drones in the background.*

CONCESSIONS GIRL

Kin I help ya?

*Travis rests his elbow on the counter, looking at the girl. He is obvi-
ously trying to be friendly – no easy task for him. God knows he
needs a friend.*

TRAVIS

What is your name? My name is Travis.

CONCESSIONS GIRL

Awh, come off it, pal.

TRAVIS

No, I'm serious, really . . .

CONCESSIONS GIRL

Ya want me to call da boss? Huh? That what you want?

TRAVIS

No, no, it's all right. I'll have a big Coca-Cola – without ice – and a large buttered popcorn, and . . .
(*pointing*)
. . . some of them chocolate-covered malted milk balls . . ., and ju-jukes, a box. They last.

CONCESSIONS GIRL

We don't have ju-jukes. We don't have Coca-Cola. We only got Royal Crown Cola.

TRAVIS

That's fine.

CONCESSIONS GIRL

That's a dollar forty-seven.

Travis lays two dollar bills on the counter.

Inside the theater auditorium.

Slight timecut. Travis is sitting in the theater, drinking his Royal Crown Cola, eating his popcorn and milk balls. His eyes are fixed on the screen. A male voice emanates from the screen.

MALE MOVIE VOICE (O.S.)

Come here, bitch. I'm gonna split you in half.

Movie voice yields to Travis's monotone narration.

TRAVIS (V.O.)
Twelve hours of work and I still cannot sleep. The days
dwindle on for ever and do not end.

WE MEET BETSY

Exterior of Charles Palantine campaign headquarters.

*The headquarters of the 'New Yorkers for Charles Palantine for Pres-
ident Committee,' located at the corner of 58th Street and Broadway,
are festooned in traditional red, white, and blue banners, ribbons,
and signs.*

*One large sign proclaims 'Palantine.' Another sign reads 'Register for
New York Primary, July 20.' The smiling middle-aged face of
Charles Palantine keeps watch over the bustling pedestrians.*

It is late afternoon.

*Inside headquarters, a variety of young workers joke and chatter as
they labor through stacks of papers. The room is pierced with the
sound of ringing phones.*

*Seen from a distance – the only way Travis can see them – these are
America's chosen youth: healthy, energetic, well-groomed, attractive,
all recruited from the bucolic fields of Massachusetts and Connecti-
cut.*

*The camera favors Betsy, about twenty-five, an extremely attractive
woman sitting at the reception desk between two phones and several
stacks of papers. Her attractions, however, are more than skin deep.
Beneath that Cover Girl facial there is a keen, though highly spe-
cialized, sensibility: her eyes scan every man who passes her desk as
her mind computes his desirability: political, intellectual, sexual,
emotional, material. Simple pose and status do not impress her; she
seeks out the extraordinary qualities in men. She is, in other words, a
star-fucker of the highest order.*

*Betsy, putting down the phone, calls Tom, a lanky, amiable, and
modishly long-haired campaign worker, over to her desk.*

                               BETSY
Tom.

Tom is pleasant and good-looking, but lacks those special qualities
which interest Betsy. He gets nowhere with Betsy – yet he keeps try-
ing. Just another of those routine office flirtations which pass the
hours and free the fantasies.

Tom, come here a moment.

He walks over.

I think this canvas report is about ready to go out. Check
it out with Andy, and if he OKs it, have a copy made for
the campaign headquarters in every county.
                            (*pause*)
And don't forget to add the new photo releases.

                               TOM
The senator's White Paper is almost ready, Bets. Should
we wait for that?

                               BETSY
Andy usually just sends those to the national media. The
local press doesn't know what to do with a position paper
until UPI and AP tell them anyway.

                               TOM
I think we should try to get maximum coverage for this
new mandatory welfare program. Push the issue.

                               BETSY
                     (*as if instructing a child*)
First push the man, then the issue. Senator Palantine is
first of all a dynamic man, an intelligent, interesting, fascinating man.

                               TOM
You forgot 'sexy.'

                               BETSY
No, I didn't forget 'sexy.'

TOM

Just didn't get around to it, huh?

BETSY

Oh, Tom, please.

TOM

Well, for Christsakes, you sound like you're selling . . . I don't know what . . . cars . . . not issues.

BETSY

Have you ever wondered why *CBS News* has the highest ratings?

TOM

More people watch it.

BETSY

All right, forget it if you're not going to be serious.

TOM

No, c'mon, I'm listening. I was just . . .

BETSY

Just what?

TOM

Kidding around . . . you know, fun.

Betsy looks toward the street, then back at Tom.

BETSY

Maybe if you'd try thinking once in a while, you'd get somewhere.

TOM

With who?

BETSY

All right, now. You want to know why CBS has the highest ratings? You think their news is any different from NBC, ABC? It's all the same news. Same stories. Same *order* usually. What, you thought they had good news for people, right? You thought that's why people watched CBS?

I'll tell you why people watch CBS. Cronkite. The man.
You got it? Not the news, not the issues, the man. If Wal-
ter Cronkite told people to eat soap, they'd do it. We *are*
selling cars, goddamn it.

*Her attention is being distracted by something she sees across the
street. She puts on her glasses and looks out across the street again.*

                          TOM
Well, if Cronkite's so great, why don't we run *him* instead?

                         BETSY
That's the last. The finish. Period. Some people can learn.
Some people can't. And you wonder why we never get
serious –

                          TOM
Sure we could run him. You realize he's already president
of his block association?

                         BETSY
                 (*looks across street again*)
Have you been noticing anything strange?

                          TOM
No, why?

                         BETSY
Why's that taxi driver across the street been staring at us?

                          TOM
What taxi driver?

                         BETSY
That taxi driver. The one that's been sitting there.

                          TOM
How long has he been there?

                         BETSY
I don't know – but it feels like a long time.

*Travis's cold, piercing eyes stare out from his cab, parked across the
street from the Palantine headquarters. He is like a lone wolf watch-*

*ing the warm camp fires of civilization from a distance. A thin red
dot glows from his cigarette. Tom exchanges Travis's gaze.*

TOM
(*determined*)
Well, I'll go out and ask him.

*As he walks toward the front door, Betsy's eyes alternate between
him and the position where Travis sits.*

*Tom strides out the front door and walks briskly out of the Palantine
headquarters, across the street toward Travis's taxi. Travis spots Tom
walking toward him and quickly starts up his cab, then squeals off
in a burst of billowing exhaust.*

Tom watches the speeding taxi quizzically.

Travis's taxi continues down Broadway.

FURTHER THOUGHTS

Inside Travis's apartment.

*Travis lies on his mattress, staring at the ceiling. He is fully clothed
and appears deep in thought.*

*Near his mattress rest several medications: a large bottle of vitamin
pills, two smaller bottles of pills, a bottle of peach-flavored brandy.*

TRAVIS (V.O.)
All my life needed was a sense of direction, a sense of
some place to go. I do not believe one should devote his
life to morbid self-attention, but should become a person
like other people.

Another day. Late afternoon.

Travis's taxi is driving down Broadway with the 'Off Duty' sign on.

*Tracking shot down Broadway. Camera stops at Palantine cam-
paign headquarters. A few workers remain in the office. Betsy's desk
is vacant.*

Fifth Avenue. The same afternoon.

Camera tracks with crowded mass of Manhattanites as they ooze through the sidewalks toward their various destinations. Individuals are indiscernible: it is simply a congested mass.

> I first saw her at Palantine Campaign Headquarters at 58th and Broadway. She was wearing a yellow dress, answering the phone at her desk.

Suddenly: out of the congested human mass, in slowing motion, appears the slender figure of Betsy, in a stylish yellow dress. The crowd parts like the Red Sea, and there she is: walking all alone, untouched by the crowd, suspended in space and time.

> She appeared like an angel out of this open sewer. Out of this filthy mass. She is alone: they cannot touch her.

Inside Travis's apartment.

Travis is at the table, writing in his diary.

Close-up: his stubby pencil rests on the word 'her.'

SMALL TALK IN A GREASY SPOON

It is 3.30 in the morning in a bacon-shaped all-night West Side restaurant. The thick smell hangs in the air – fried grease, smoke, sweat, regurgitated wine.

Whatever doesn't flush away in New York at night turns up in places like this. A burly grease-stained cook stands over the grill. A junkie shuffles from one side of the door to another. Slouched over the small four-person formica tables are several well-dressed blacks (too well-dressed for this time and place), a cluster of street people, and a lost old coot who hangs on to his cup of coffee as if it were his last possession.

The restaurant, brightly lit, perfectly conveys the image of urban plasticity – without the slightest hint of an accompanying cleanliness. Toward the rear of the restaurant sit three cabbies: Wizard, a worn man of about fifty, Dough-Boy, younger family man, Charlie T, fortyish, black.

Wizard is telling Dough-Boy a story. Charlie T, his elbows propped against the table top, is not listening. He stares silently down at a plate of cold scrambled eggs and a Racing Forum. *His eyes may not be open.*

WIZARD
First she did her make-up. You know, I hate it when they do that. I mean she does the whole works, the mascara, the eye-shadow, the lipstick, the rouge.

DOUGH-BOY
Not rouge. Blush-On, they call it.

WIZARD
The kind with a brush?

Travis appears at the door. He has to push aside the junkie in order to enter, without making physical contact – something Travis would not relish. He may be repulsed with these people and this place, but he is too much a part of this to let his feelings rise to the surface.

Wizard gives Travis a perfunctory wave.

Travis.

TRAVIS
Hey, Wizard.

Travis straddles a seat at the table. Dough-Boy gives Travis something between a wink and an eye-twitch and says:

DOUGH-BOY
Yeah, that's Blush-On. My wife uses it.

WIZARD
(*ironic*)
Ask Travis. He's the ladies' man.

Travis shrugs and motions for a cup of coffee.

Well, whatever the fuck it is, she used it. And then the spray perfume. You know, the real sweet kind – and, on top of that, get this, right when we're crossing the Triboro bridge – she changes her pantyhose!

DOUGH-BOY

No.

Travis turns his head. He appears not be interested, but is.

WIZARD

Yeah.

DOUGH-BOY

Could you see anything?

WIZARD

Well, she was trying to keep her skirt down, sort of, you know. But it was pretty obvious what she was doing. I mean, Christ, it was rush hour and the traffic's practically standing still.

DOUGH-BOY

What did you do?

WIZARD

Threw on the emergency, jumped the seat and fucked her brains out – what do you think!

They laugh.

What do I have to do? Draw you a picture?

DOUGH-BOY

Yeah.

WIZARD

What was I supposed to do? I was watching in the rear-view. You know, just checkin' traffic.

DOUGH-BOY

She saw you watching?

A waitress brings Travis's coffee and a glass of water. He asks for a cheeseburger.

WIZARD

Sure. What do you think? She wanted to get out of the cab. I said, 'Look, you're in the middle of the fucking bridge . . .'

DOUGH-BOY

You said that? You said 'fuckin'' to her?

WIZARD

Well, I said, 'Lady, please, we're on a bridge . . .'

DOUGH-BOY

And what happened?

Travis awaits Wizard's answer.

WIZARD

She stayed in the cab, what's she gonna do? But she stiffed me. A real skunk.

DOUGH-BOY

A real skunk.

Wizard realizes Travis and Dough-Boy may not have met.

WIZARD
(*paternal*)
Travis, you know Dough-Boy, Charlie T?

Charlie T nods sleepily. Travis indicates he knows Dough-Boy.

DOUGH-BOY

Yeah. We went to Harvard together.

He laughs.

WIZARD

We call him Dough-Boy 'cause he likes the dollars. He'll chase a buck straight into Jersey.

DOUGH-BOY

Look who's talking?
(*gestures around table*)
Who else would stay up all night to catch the morning rush hour?

Travis sips his coffee. Charlie T's eyelids slip shut.

WIZARD
(*to Travis*)

So howsit?

TRAVIS
(*in a monotone*)

Some fleet driver for Bell just got cut up. Just heard it on
the radio.

DOUGH-BOY

Stick-up?

TRAVIS

No, just some crazy fucker. Cut half his ear off.

DOUGH-BOY

Where?

TRAVIS

In the Jungle. 122nd.

*Travis's eyes turn toward the restaurant's other patrons. There are
three street people sitting at a table. One guy, stoned, stares straight
ahead. A raggedly attractive girl rests her head on the shoulder of the
other, a heavily bearded young man with a headband. They kiss
and tease each other, momentarily lost in their separate world.*

*Travis watches the hippie couple closely, his feelings sharply divided
between cultural contempt and morose jealousy. Why should these people enjoy the love and intimacy that has always eluded him? He must
enjoy these schizoid emotions, because his eyes dwell on the couple.*

DOUGH-BOY (O.S.)
(*changing the subject*)

You run all over town, don't you, Travis?

WIZARD
(*referring to 122nd Street*)

Fuckin' Mau Mau land, that's what it is.

Travis turns back to his companions.

TRAVIS

Huh?

DOUGH-BOY

I mean, you handle some pretty rough traffic, huh?

TRAVIS
(*catching on*)

I have.

DOUGH-BOY

You carry a piece? You need one?

TRAVIS

Nah.

(*pause*)

I suppose not.

The waitress slaps down a smudge-marked glass of water and a cheeseburger plate that looks more like a shrunken head on a serving platter.

DOUGH-BOY

Well, you ever need one, I know a feller that kin getcha a real nice deal. Lotsa shit around.

WIZARD

The cops and company raise hell if they find out.

Travis drops two Alka-Seltzers into his glass of water.

DOUGH-BOY

Truck drivers bring up Harlem Specials that blow up in your hand. But this guy don't deal no shit. Just quality. If you ever need anything, I can put you in touch.

WIZARD

For a fee.

DOUGH-BOY

For a fee.

WIZARD

I never use mine. But it's a good thing to have. Just as a threat.

> DOUGH-BOY
> (*getting up*)
> Well, if there's this many hackies *inside*, there must be lots
> of fares *outside*. And I'm gonna go hustle 'em.

> WIZARD
> What ya gonna do with all that money, Dough-Boy?

> DOUGH-BOY
> Support my kids. Can you dig it?
> (*pause*)
> Nice to meet ya, Travis. So long, Wizard.
> (*nods to Charlie T*)
> Say hello to Malcolm X for me.

*Charlie T remains unmoved: he is sleeping. Dough-Boy exits. Travis
smiles perfunctorily, then looks back at Wizard. They really don't
have much to talk about, and the Wizard doesn't care to manufac-
ture any more conversation.*

Travis scans the greasy spoon: the scene is unchanged.

BETSY MEETS TRAVIS BICKLE

Exterior of the Palantine headquarters – another day. Traffic passes.

*Inside the Palantine headquarters. Tom and Betsy are talking. She
takes out a cigarette. He takes out matches to light it.*

> BETSY
> Try holding the match like this.

> TOM
> This has gotta be a game, right?

> BETSY
> (*putting on her glasses*)
> This I gotta see.

> TOM
> (*burning fingers*)
> Ouch!

BETSY
(*giggling*)
Oh, are you all right?

TOM
I'm great. Always set my fingers on fire. Nothing to it.
Want to see another trick? I do this thing with my nose.

BETSY
No. I just wanted to see if you could light it that way. The
guy at the news-stand can.

TOM
Ah, yes, the guy at the news-stand, Mr Asbestos . . .

BETSY
He happens to be missing fingers. I first noticed when –

TOM
Is he Italian?

BETSY
No, why?

TOM
You sure he's not Italian?

BETSY
He's *black*, OK?

TOM
Well, if he had been Italian, they could have been shot off.
Sometimes the mob does that to teach guys a lesson. If
they blow a job or something.

BETSY
As I said, he isn't Italian. Besides, I thought they just
killed them.

TOM
Don't be naive. They can't kill everybody. They have different punishments for different things. Like, if they kill a
stool pigeon, they leave a canary on the body. It's symbolic.

BETSY

Why don't they leave a pigeon instead of a canary?

TOM

I don't know. Maybe they don't leave a canary. Don't be
technical. What I'm saying is if this news-stand guy's Italian and his fingers are gone, maybe he's a thief.

BETSY

First, he's not Italian. Second, he's not a thief. I noticed
the fingers when he was getting my change – the right
change. Two of his fingers are missing. Just stubs. Like
they were blown away. I was putting my change in my
purse when I saw him get out a cigarette. I couldn't help
watching. I was dying to see how he'd light it.

TOM

With the other hand, right?

BETSY

No, stupid. With the stubs. That's the whole point.

TOM

I know that guy. His hand looks like a paw. An old black
guy, the news-stand at –

BETSY

No, this is young – well, I'm never sure how old black
people are – but, anyway, he isn't old. That's for sure.

TOM

Show me how he did that again.

Across the street from the headquarters.

*Travis is striding briskly across Broadway toward the Palantine
headquarters.*

*He is dressed the best we have seen him: his trousers (not jeans) are
pressed, his boots shined, his hair combed. Under his Army jacket he
wears a freshly laundered shirt and Ivy League tie. He drops his cigarette, steps on it, and walks in. Watching Travis enter Palantine's*

headquarters, we are again surprised to realize that Travis is really quite attractive. His deformities are psychological, not physical. He believes he is cursed, and therefore he is.

Travis walks briskly into the office and heads toward Betsy's desk. Tom walks over to greet him, but Travis ignores him.

> TRAVIS
> (*at Betsy's desk*)

I want to volunteer.

As the camera examines Travis's face more closely, one can see the hollowness wrought by lack of sleep and an insufficient diet.

> TOM
> (*interrupting*)

If you'll come this way.

Travis elbows Tom off.

> TRAVIS
> (*to Betsy*)

No. I want to volunteer to *you.*

> TOM
> (*under his voice*)

Bets.

Betsy waves Tom off with a short gesture, indicating everything is OK. He walks away.

> BETSY
> (*curious*)

And why is that?

Travis is on his best behavior. He smiles slightly.

> TRAVIS

Because you are the most beautiful woman I have ever seen.

Betsy is momentarily taken back, but pleased. Travis's presence has a definite sexual charge. He has those star qualities Betsy looks for: she senses there is something special about the young man who stands before her. And then, too, there is that disarming smile. He is, as Betsy would say, 'fascinating.'

> BETSY
> (*smiling*)

Is that so?

> (*pause*)

But what do you think of Charles Palantine?

> TRAVIS
> (*his mind elsewhere*)

Who, Ma'am?

> BETSY

Charles Palantine. The man you want to volunteer to help elect President.

> TRAVIS

Oh, I think he's a wonderful man. Make a great, great President.

> BETSY

You want to canvass?

> TRAVIS

Yes, Ma'am.

Betsy is interviewing Travis, but she is also teasing him a little, leading him on in a gentle feminine way.

> BETSY

How do you feel about Senator Palantine's stand on welfare?

This takes Travis back a bit. He obviously doesn't have the slightest idea what Palantine's stand on welfare is; in fact, he doesn't have any ideas about politics whatsoever. Travis thinks a moment, then improvises an answer.

> TRAVIS

Welfare, Ma'am? I think the Senator's right. People should work for a living. I do. Every day. I like to work. Get those old coots off welfare and make 'em work for a change.

Betsy does a subtle double-take: this isn't exactly Palantine's position on welfare. She remains intrigued by Travis.

BETSY

Well, that's not exactly what the Senator has proposed. You might not want to canvass, but there is plenty of other work we need done: office work, filing, poster hanging.

TRAVIS

I'm a good worker, Betsy Ma'am, a real good worker.

BETSY
(*gesturing*)
If you talk to Tom, he'll assign you to something.

TRAVIS

If you don't mind, Ma'am, I'd rather work for you.

BETSY

Well, we're *all* working tonight.

TRAVIS

Well, Betsy Ma'am, I drive a taxi at night.

BETSY

Well, then, what is it you *exactly* want to do?

TRAVIS
(*bolstering courage*)
If you don't mind, Ma'am, I'd be mighty pleased if you'd go out and have some coffee and pie with me.

Betsy doesn't quite know what to make of Travis. She is curious, intrigued, tantalized. Like a moth, she draws closer to the flame.

BETSY

Why?

TRAVIS

Well, Betsy Ma'am, I drive by this place here in my taxi many times a day. And I watch you sitting here at this big long desk with these telephones, and I say to myself, that's a lonely girl. She needs a friend. And I'm gonna be her friend.

He smiles.

Travis rarely smiles, but when he does his whole face glows. It is as if he is able to tap an inner reserve of charm unknown even to himself. Betsy is completely disarmed.

> BETSY
>
> I don't know . . .

> TRAVIS
>
> It's just to the corner, Ma'am. In broad daytime. Nothing can happen. I'll be there to protect you.

> BETSY
> *(smiles, relenting)*
>
> All right. All right. I'm taking a break at four o'clock. If you're here then we'll go to the corner and have some coffee and pie.

> TRAVIS
>
> Oh, I appreciate that, Betsy Ma'am. I'll be here at four o'clock exactly.
> *(pause)*
> And . . . ah . . . Betsy . . .

> BETSY
>
> Yes?

> TRAVIS
>
> My name is Travis.

> BETSY
>
> Thank you, Travis.

Travis nods, turns, and exits.

Tom, who has been watching this interchange with a pseudo-stand-offish (actually jealous) air, steps over to Betsy. His manner demands some sort of explanation of what she was doing.

Betsy simply shrugs – it's really none of his business.

> I'm just going to find out what the cabbies are thinking.

COFFEE-SHOP RENDEZVOUS

Travis is pacing back and forth on Broadway just beyond the Palantine headquarters. He checks his watch.

TRAVIS (V.O.)
April 26, 1972. Four o'clock p.m. I took Betsy to the Mayfair coffee shop on Broadway . . .

Travis and Betsy are sitting in a booth of a small New York coffee shop. They have both been served coffee; Travis is nervously turning his cup around in his hands.

The waitress brings their orders: apple pie for Travis, fruit compote for Betsy.

I had black coffee and apple pie with a slice of melted yellow cheese. I think that was a good selection. Betsy had coffee and a fruit salad dish. She could have had anything she wanted.

Betsy's conversation interrupts Travis.

BETSY
We've signed up 15,000 Palantine volunteers in New York so far. The organizational problems are becoming just staggering.

TRAVIS
I know what you mean. I've got the same problems. I just can't get things organized. Little things, I mean. Like my room, my possessions. I should get one of those signs that says, 'One of These Days I'm Gonna Get Organezizied.'

Travis contorts his mouth to match his mispronunciation, then breaks into a big, friendly, infectious grin. The very sight of it makes one's heart pound.

Betsy cannot help but be caught up in Travis's grin. Travis's contagious, quicksilver moods cause her to say:

BETSY
(*laughing*)
Travis, I never ever met *any*body like you before.

TRAVIS
I can believe that.

BETSY
Where *do* you live?

TRAVIS
(*evasive*)
Oh, uptown. You know. Some joint. It ain't much.

BETSY
So why did you decide to drive a taxi at *night*?

TRAVIS
I had a regular job for a while, days. You know, doin' this,
doin' that. But I didn't have anything to do at *night*. I got
kinda lonely, you know, just wanderin' around. So I
decided to work nights. It ain't good to be alone, you
know.

BETSY
After this job, I'm looking *forward* to being alone for a
while.

TRAVIS
Yeah, well . . .
(*pause*)
In a cab you get to meet people. You meet lotsa people.
It's good for you.

BETSY
What kind of people?

TRAVIS
Just people people, you know. Just people.
(*pause*)
Had a dead man once.

BETSY

Really?

TRAVIS

He'd been shot. I didn't know that. He just crawled into the back seat, said, 'West 45th Street,' and conked out.

BETSY

What did you do?

TRAVIS

I shut the meter off, for one thing. I knew I wasn't going to get paid. Then I dropped him off at the cop shop. They took him.

BETSY

That's really something.

TRAVIS

Oh, you see lots of freaky stuff in a cab. Especially when the moon's out.

BETSY

The moon?

TRAVIS

The full moon. One night I had three or four weirdos in a row and I looked up and, sure enough, there it was – the full moon.

Betsy laughs.

Oh, yeah. People will do anything in front of a taxi driver. I mean *anything*. People too cheap to rent a hotel room, people scoring dope, people shooting up, people who want to embarrass you.
          (*a bitterness emerges*)
It's like you're not even there, not even a person. Nobody knows you.

Betsy cuts Travis's bitterness short.

BETSY

C'mon, Travis. It's not that bad. I take lots of taxis.

TRAVIS

I know. I could have picked you up.

BETSY

Huh?

TRAVIS

Late one night. About three. At the Plaza.

BETSY

Three in the morning? I don't think so. I have to go to bed early. I work *days*. It must have been somebody else.

TRAVIS

No. It was you. You had some manila folders and a pink bag from Saks.

Betsy, realizing Travis remembers her precisely, scrambles for a polite rationale for her behavior.

BETSY

You're right! Now I remember! It was after the Western regional planners were in town and the meeting went on late. The next day I was completely bushed. It was unbelievable.

TRAVIS

If it wasn't for a drunk I would have picked you up. He wanted to go to the DMZ.

BETSY

The DMZ?

TRAVIS

South Bronx. The worst. I tried to ditch him, but he was already in the cab, so I had to take him. That's the law. Otherwise I would have picked you up.

BETSY

That would have been quite a coincidence.

TRAVIS

You'd be surprised how often you see the same people, get the same fare. People have patterns. They do more or less the same things every day. I can tell.

BETSY

Well, I don't go to the Plaza every night.

TRAVIS

I didn't mean you. But just ordinary people. A guy I know – Dough-Boy – met his wife that way. They got to talking. She said she usually caught the bus so he started picking her up at the bus stop, taking her home with the flag up.

BETSY

That's very romantic. Some of your fares must be interesting. See any stars, politicians, deliver any babies yet?

TRAVIS
(embarrassed)

Well, no . . . not really . . . had some famous people in the cab . . .
(remembering)
I got this guy who makes lasers. Not regular lasers, not the big kind. Little lasers, pocket-sized, small enough to clip to your belt like a transistor radio, like a gun, you know. Like a ray gun. Zap.

BETSY
(laughs)

What hours do you work?

TRAVIS

I work a single, which means there's no replacement – no second man on the cab. Six to six, sometimes eight. Seventy-two hours a week.

BETSY
(amazed)

You mean you work seventy-two hours a week?

TRAVIS

Sometimes seventy-six or eighty. Sometimes I squeeze a few more hours in the morning. Eighty miles a day, a hundred miles a night.

BETSY

You must be rich.

TRAVIS
(*big affectionate smile*)

It keeps ya busy.

BETSY

You know what you remind me of?

TRAVIS

What?

BETSY

That song by Kris Kristofferson, where it says, 'He's a prophet and a pusher, partly truth, partly fiction, a walking contradiction.'

She smiles.

TRAVIS
(*uneasy*)

I'm no pusher, Betsy. Honest. I never have pushed.

BETSY

I didn't mean that, Travis. Just the part about the contradiction.

TRAVIS
(*more at ease*)

Oh. Who was that again?

BETSY

The singer?

TRAVIS

Yeah. I don't follow music too much.

BETSY
(*slowly*)
Kris Kristofferson.

Travis looks at Betsy intently and they exchange smiles.

INCIDENT IN A RECORD SHOP

Travis is walking confusedly around Sam Goody's at midday, obviously unable to locate what he desires.

He is lost among the hip, young intellectual types that populate the store. He watches the stylish, attractive female assistant, unable to come right out and request what he desires.

A young sales girl sees his plight, walks over, and asks if he needs any help. Travis inaudibly says a name to her, although the name is obviously Kristofferson's.

The sales girl digs out Kristofferson's Silver-Tongued Devil *album for him.*

Travis says something else to the sales girl and she goes off to gift-wrap the album.

Travis emerges from the record store, the brightly gift-wrapped album proudly tucked under his arm.

A NIGHT BEHIND THE WHEEL

A lengthy point-of-view shot from Travis's vantage-point behind the wheel.

We see the city as Travis sees it. The front windscreen is a little dirty, the lit-up meter juts up at the lower right screen. The intercom crackles with static and messages.

The lights turn green; we take off with a start. A short first gear – quick shift – a long second gear. The cab eases to the right of the street, checking out prospective fares.

Our eyes scan the long line of pedestrians. The regulars – bums, junkies, tourists, hookers, homosexuals, hippies – they mean nothing now. They only blend into the sidewalks and lighted storefronts. Our eyes now concentrate on those that step away from the curb – is that man hailing a cab or scratching his head?

In the next block there are perhaps three, four fares – quick gas-up through this yellow light – brake sharply – check the action. The first: tourists, nickel tippers – let the next guy pick them up. Let the second go also, the third – there's a live fare: a middle-aged local woman, short fare to the East Side, good tip.

We pull over to the curb, waiting for her to get in. It is a long wait – a black streetwalker crosses in front of the cab. We focus on (as Travis would) a young couple embracing in the distance. As we travel, we hear Travis's random thoughts about selecting fares and tips.

TRAVIS (V.O.)

You work at night, you get an instinct. You can smell them. The big tippers, the stiffs, the trouble-makers. Quarter is good tip for Manhattan. Queens is better, Brooklyn the best. Go for the guy with suitcases. The rich are the worst tippers, Hooks are lousy. Spooks are OK, but they don't live on Park Avenue, after all.

The meter is activated: $0.60 registers. Tick, tick, tick. A quick glance shows the woman is now seated. She says softly, '192 East 89.' We take off with another jolt. Cross back up 9th Avenue, then cut through the park.

We're zooming up 9th Avenue; how many green lights can we string together? Somebody steps out to hail the cab, but quickly steps back again. The meter is up to $0.90. It'll be a $1.40 fare.

Now through the park and we're almost there. Check the numbers – 134 – 140. End of the block. The fare comes to $1.40.

Check back mirror – she's getting out two bills. Two quarters and a dime change. Tip'll be either 0.25 or 0.35.

The tip comes back: 35¢; a good tip. Good lady. We take off again with a jolt.

This is Travis's world: dark side streets, garish glaring main streets, quick glances, quicker evaluations – a dozen instantaneous decisions a minute. Are these people, are these objects?

Travis's taxi speeds down a darkened street. Travis lets off a fare and pulls into line at the Plaza.

> I called Betsy again at her office, and she said maybe we could go to a movie together after she gets off work tomorrow. That's my day off. At first she hesitated, but I called her again and she agreed.
> > (*pause*)
> Betsy. Betsy what? I forgot to ask her last name again. Damn. I've got to remember stuff like that.

Travis's thoughts are with Betsy as three men enter Travis's cab. He activates the meter and pulls off.

MAN (O.S.)
> St Regis Hotel.

Travis checks the mirror. Scanning across the back seat, he recognizes the middle passenger. It is Charles Palantine, candidate for President. He must have left the hotel shortly after Betsy.

Tom, seated on the jump seat, checks his watch and speaks deferentially to Palantine.

TOM
> It's 12.30 now. You'll have fifteen minutes before the actual luncheon begins.

Palantine nods as his assistant picks up the thread of an earlier conversation.

ASSISTANT
> I don't think we have to worry about anybody here committing themselves until things start coming in from California.

Travis puts out his cigarette.

TRAVIS
(*interrupting*)
Say, aren't you Charles Palantine, the candidate?

PALANTINE
(*only mildly irritated*)
Yes, I am.

TRAVIS
Well, I'm one of your biggest supporters, I tell everybody that comes in this cab that they should vote for you.

PALANTINE
(*pleased; glances to check Travis's license*)
Why, thank you, Travis.

TRAVIS
I'm sure you'll win, sir. Everybody I know is going to vote for you.
(*a pause*)
I was going to put one of your stickers on my taxi but the company said it was against their policy.

PALANTINE
(*pleasant*)
I'll tell you, Travis, I've learned more about this country sitting in taxi-cabs than in the boardroom of General Motors.

TOM
(*joking*)
And in some other places too . . .

Palantine, his assistant, and Tom all laugh.

Palantine, quickly reassuming his canditatorial mien, speaks to Travis.

PALANTINE
Travis, what single thing would *you* want the next President of this country to do most?

TRAVIS

I don't know, sir. I don't follow political issues much.

PALANTINE

There must be something . . .

TRAVIS
(*thinks*)

Well, he should clean up this city here. It's full of filth and scum; scum and filth. It's like an open sewer. Sometimes I can hardly take it. Some days I go out and smell it, then I get headaches that just stay and never go away. We need a President that would clean up this whole mess. Flush it out.

Palantine is not a Hubert Humphrey-type professional bullshitter, and Travis's intense reply stops him dead in his tracks. He is forced to fall back on a stock answer, but he tries to give it some meaning.

PALANTINE
(*after a pause*)

I know what you mean, Travis, and it's not going to be easy. We're going to have to make some radical changes.

TRAVIS
(*turning the wheel*)

Damn straight.

Travis's taxi pulls up in front of the Barclay Hotel.

Palantine and Tom get out of the cab. The assistant stays in the back seat a moment to pay Travis.

Palantine looks in the front window of cab momentarily and nods goodbye to Travis.

PALANTINE

Nice talking to you, Travis.

TRAVIS
(*calling back*)

Thank you, sir. You're a good man, sir.

Travis's taxi departs.

Palantine and assistants walk up carpet to the hotel.

Close-up of Palantine as he stops, turns back, and watches Travis's departing taxi.

Palantine turns back and ascends the hotel steps with his assistants.

DATE NIGHT

Manhattan street. Early evening.

Travis, dressed up to the eyeballs, walks brightly down the sidewalk. His face is freshly shaved, his hair combed, his tie straightened.

He pauses in a store window to check his appearance. Under his arm he carries the gift-wrapped Kristofferson album.

Outside Palantine headquarters Betsy, smartly dressed, waves good-bye to another campaign worker and walks out the door to greet Travis.

A short while later, Travis and Betsy are walking down Broadway toward Times Square. Betsy does not let their bodies touch as they walk, although Travis contemplates edging closer to her.

Betsy has opened the package and is admiring the record – or, rather, Travis's sentiment behind giving it.

Travis looks round with pride: this is a moment to savor in his life – one of the few.

BETSY

You didn't have to spend your money –

TRAVIS
(interrupting)

Hell, what else can I do with it all?

Betsy notices that the seal on the record has not been broken.

BETSY

Travis, you haven't even played the record?

TRAVIS
(*evasive*)
Yeah, well, my stereo player is broke. But I'm sure the record is OK.

BETSY
Your stereo broke? God, I could hardly stand that. I *live* on music.

TRAVIS
I don't follow music much. I'd like to though.
(*second thought*)
Honest.

BETSY
(*pointing to album*)
So you haven't heard this record yet?

TRAVIS
No.
(*sly smile*)
I thought maybe you could play it for me on your player.

Betsy's face backtracks a bit. Maybe she was wrong to go out with this fellow she doesn't know.

She makes a polite laugh.

Later. Travis and Betsy are in Times Square, turning the corner from Broadway to 42nd Street. Travis carries the album under his arm.

They approach the garish marquee of a large midtown porno theater advertising The Swedish Marriage Manual. *The box-office is flanked on both sides by glass cages filled with explicit publicity stills. Offending portions have been blocked out with black tape.*

Travis steps over to the window and buys two $5 tickets. Betsy, befuddled, watches him. She doesn't know what to say.

Travis returns with the tickets.

Betsy still has not fully comprehended what is happening.

BETSY

What are you doing?

TRAVIS
(*innocent*)

I bought a couple of tickets.

BETSY

But this is a porno movie.

TRAVIS

No, these are the kind that couples go to. They're not like the other movies. All kinds of couples go. Honest. I've seen them.

Travis seems confused. He is so much a part of his own world, he fails to comprehend another's world. Compared to the movies he sees, this is respectable. But then there's also something that Travis could not even acknowledge, much less admit: that he really wants to get this pure white girl into that dark porno theater.

He makes an awkward gesture to escort Betsy into the theater. Betsy looks at the tickets, at the theater, at Travis. She mentally shakes her head and walks toward the turnstile. She thinks to herself: 'What the hell. What can happen?' She's always been curious about these pictures anyway, and – like all women, no matter how intelligent – she's been raised not to offend her date. A perverse logic which applies even more in offsetting circumstances like these.

Inside the theater. Travis escorts Betsy to an empty center row. Travis was right. Couples do go to films like this. There are at least six or seven other men with their bewigged 'dates.' Travis settles into his familiar porno theater slouch. Betsy looks curiously from side to side.

On screen, a conservatively dressed middle-aged woman is speaking in Swedish about the importance of a healthy sex life in a happy marriage. Subtitles translate her words. Then, without warning, there is a direct cut to a couple copulating on a sterile table-like bed.

Travis watches intently. The color, however, is slowly draining from Betsy's cheeks. One thought fills her mind: 'What am I doing here?'

(*to himself*)

Damn.

BETSY

What's wrong?

TRAVIS

I forgot to get the Coca-Cola.

That does it. Betsy just looks at him for a moment, then gets up and starts to leave. Travis, confused, hustles after her. He follows her out of the theater.

On the sidewalk Travis catches up with her.

Where are you going?

BETSY

I'm leaving.

TRAVIS

What do you mean?

Betsy looks at Travis, trying to understand him.

BETSY

These are not the kind of movies I go to.

TRAVIS

Well, I don't follow movies too much . . .

BETSY

You mean these are the only kind of movies you go to?

The ticket girl watches expressionlessly from the booth.

TRAVIS

This is sort of high class . . .

BETSY

I mean porno movies.

TRAVIS
(*hesitant*)

Well . . . mostly . . .

BETSY

My God!

TRAVIS

We can go to another movie if you like, I don't care. I got
money. There's plenty . . .

*Travis gestures toward the long row of 42nd Street marquees, but is
interrupted by Betsy.*

BETSY

If you just wanted to fuck, why didn't you just come right
out and say it?

*Travis is flabbergasted by Betsy's blunt language. His arm still ges-
tures toward the marquees, his lips continue to move, but words do
not come out.*

*Unable to respond to Betsy's question, Travis picks up where he left
off.*

TRAVIS

There's plenty of movies around here. I haven't seen any
of them, but I'm sure they're good.

BETSY

No, Travis. You're a sweet guy and all that, but I think this
is it. I'm going home.

TRAVIS
(*interrupting*)
You mean you don't want to go to a movie?
(*pause*)
There's plenty of movies around here.

BETSY

No, I don't feel so good. We're just two very different
kinds of people, that's all.

TRAVIS
(*puzzled*)
Huh?

BETSY

It's very simple. You go your way, I'll go mine. Thanks anyway, Travis.

TRAVIS

But . . . Betsy . . .

BETSY

I'm getting a taxi.

She walks to the curb.

TRAVIS
(*following her*)

But your record?

BETSY

Keep it.

TRAVIS

Can I call you?

Betsy looks for a cab.

(*tender*)
Please, Betsy, I bought it for *you.*

Betsy looks at his sad, sweet face and relents a bit.

BETSY

All right, I'll accept the record.

She accepts the record, but quickly turns and hails a taxi.

Taxi!

A taxi quickly pulls up.

Travis feebly protests to no one in particular.

TRAVIS

But I *got* a taxi.

Betsy gives instructions to cab driver, looks briefly back at Travis, then straight ahead. Taxi speeds off.

Travis looks around helplessly: a cluster of pedestrians on the crowded street has stopped to watch the argument. Travis looks back at the woman in the porno theater box-office, who has also been following the argument.

PHONE CALLS AND FLOWERS

Inside Travis's apartment.

Travis is writing at the table. There are some new items on the table: his giant econo-size bottle of vitamins, a giant econo-size bottle of aspirins, a pint of apricot brandy, a partial loaf of cheap white bread.

On the wall behind the table hang two more items: a gag sign reading 'One of These Days I'm Gonna Get Organezizied' and an orange-and-black bumper sticker for Charles Palantine.

TRAVIS (V.O.)
May 8, 1972. My life has taken another turn again. The days move along with regularity . . .

Close-up of notebook: Travis is no longer sitting at desk. The pencil rests on the open notebook.

Later that day: Travis has pulled his straight-backed chair around and is watching his small portable TV, which rests on the upright melon crate. A cereal bowl partially filled with milk rests in his lap. He pours a couple of shots of the apricot brandy into the bowl, dips folded chunks of white bread into the mixture, and eats them. He is watching an early-evening news program. There is the sound of the TV in the background. Charles Palantine is being interviewed somewhere on the campaign trail.

. . . one day indistinguishable from the next, a long continuous chain, then suddenly – there is a change.

Betsy is walking down a midtown street when Travis suddenly appears before her. He has been waiting. Travis tries to make conversation but she doesn't listen. She motions for him to go away and keeps on walking. Travis, protesting, follows.

Inside a building. Day.

Travis speaks intensely into a wall pay-phone.

I tried to call her several times.

We hear Travis's voice on the phone:

You feeling better? You said you didn't feel so good . . .

Back to voice-over:

But after the first call, she would no longer come to the phone.

He holds the receiver in his hand. The other party has hung up.

Tracking shot across interior lower wall of Travis's apartment. Against the stark wall there is a row of wilted and dying floral arrangements. Each one of the four or five bouquets is progressively more wilted than the one closer to the door. They have been returned.

I also sent flowers with no luck. I should not dwell on such things, but set them behind me. The smell of the flowers only made me sicker. The headaches got worse. I think I've got stomach cancer. I should not complain so. 'You're only as healthy as you feel.'

A drama is acted out at Palantine headquarters: Travis, groggy and red-eyed from lack of sleep, walks into the campaign headquarters about noon.

Betsy is standing near the rear of the office; she ducks from sight when she sees Travis enter. Travis's path is cut short by Tom's large-framed body. There is no live sound.

I realize now how much she is like the others, so cold and distant. Many people are like that. Women for sure. They're like a union.

Travis tries to push his way past Tom, but Tom grabs him. Travis says something sharply to Tom and the two scuffle. Tom, by far the taller and stronger, quickly overcomes Travis, wrenching his arm behind his back.

Travis kicks and protests as Tom leads him to the front door. On the sidewalk, Travis's efforts quickly subside when Tom motions to a nearby policeman. Travis quietens down and walks off.

THE PUSSY AND THE .44

Travis is again making his way through the garish urban night. He stops for a passenger on Park Avenue, a middle-aged professorial executive.

Close-up of Travis: his face is expressionless. The man makes himself comfortable in the back seat.

> PROFESSORIAL PASSENGER
> Jackson Heights.

Travis has no intention of driving out to Jackson Heights and coming back with a fare.

> TRAVIS
> I'm off duty.

> PROFESSORIAL PASSENGER
> You mean you don't want to go out to Jackson Heights?

> TRAVIS
> No, I'm off duty.

> PROFESSORIAL PASSENGER
> Then how come your 'Off Duty' light wasn't on?

Travis switches on the 'Off Duty' light.

> TRAVIS
> It was on.
> *(gesturing toward top of taxi)*
> It just takes a while to warm up. Like a TV.

Travis doesn't budge. Professorial passenger curses to himself and gets out of cab. Travis takes off.

Travis's eyes dwell on the young hip couples coming out of an East Side movie house.

Later that night, Travis pulls over for a young (mid-twenties) man wearing a leather sports jacket.

Travis eyes his passenger in a rear-view mirror.

> YOUNG PASSENGER
>
> 417 Central Park West.

Travis's taxi speeds off.

Later, Travis's taxi slows down as it approaches 400 block of Central Park West.

Travis checks apartment numbers.

> Just pull over to the curb a moment.

Travis turns the wheel.

> Yeah, that's fine. Just sit here.

Travis waits impassively. The meter ticks away. After a long pause, the young passenger speaks:

> Cabbie, ya see that light up there on the seventh floor, three windows from this side of the building?

Camera closes in on 417 Central Park West: tracking up to the seventh floor, it moves three windows to the right.

> TRAVIS (O.S.)
>
> Yeah.

A young woman wearing a slip crosses in front of the light.

> YOUNG PASSENGER (O.S.)
>
> Ya see that woman there?

> TRAVIS (O.S.)
>
> Yeah.

> YOUNG PASSENGER (O.S.)
>
> That's my wife.
>
> > (pause)
>
> But it ain't my apartment.

(*pause*)

A nigger lives there.

(*pause*)

She left me two weeks ago. It took me this long to find out where she went.

(*pause*)

I'm gonna kill her.

Close-up of Travis's face: it is devoid of expression.

What do you think of that, cabbie?

Close-up of young passenger's face: it is gaunt, drained of blood, full of fear and anger.

Travis does not respond.

Huh?

(*pause*)

What do you think of that, huh?

Travis shrugs, gesturing toward meter.

I'm gonna kill her with a .44 Magnum pistol.

Camera returns to seventh-floor window. Woman is standing in the light.

Did you ever see what a .44 can do to a woman's face, cabbie?

(*pause*)

Did you ever see what it can do to a woman's pussy, cabbie?

Travis says nothing.

I'm going to put it right up to her, cabbie. Right in her, cabbie. You must think I'm real sick, huh? A real pervert. Sitting here and talking about a woman's pussy and a .44, huh?

Camera closes in on Travis's face: he is watching the woman in the seventh-floor window with complete and total absorption. It's the same glazed-over stare we saw in his eyes as he watched the porno movie.

THE TRAVELING SALESMAN

Brooklyn street corner. Day.

Travis stands near the corner wearing his boots, jeans, western shirt, and Army jacket.

He pulls his aspirin bottle out of his pocket, shakes three or four into his palm, pops them into his mouth, and chews.

An 'Off Duty' taxi pulls up to the curb. Travis gets in.

Dough-Boy leans back from the wheel and greets Travis as he enters.

> DOUGH-BOY
> Hey, Travis. This here's Easy Andy. He's a traveling sales-man.

In the back seat, beside Travis, sits Andy, an attractive young man of about twenty-nine. He wears a pin-striped suit, white shirt, and floral tie. His hair is modishly long.

> ANDY
> Hello, Travis.

Travis nods as the taxi speeds off.

Dough-Boy slows down near an economy hotel. Not a flophouse, but not so fancy they care what the guests do in the privacy of their rooms.

> This is fine, Dough-Boy.
> > (*to Travis*)
> Pay Dough-Boy here.

Travis pulls a twenty-dollar bill out of his pocket and gives it to Dough-Boy.

> TRAVIS
> Twenty bucks?

> DOUGH-BOY
> > (*takes bill*)
> Yeah. Hey thanks. That's real nice, Travis.

Travis and Andy get out of the cab and walk toward the hotel. Dough-Boy pulls away.

As they enter the hotel, they pass a junkie, stoned out and spread-eagled across the hood of a derelict old blue Dodge. Inside the hotel, Travis follows Andy up the worn carpeted stairs and down the hallway. Andy unlocks the door to one of the rooms. The hotel room is barren and clean; there's no sign anyone is staying in it. The fire-escape is appropriately near. Andy locks the door behind them, steps over to the closet, unlocks it and pulls out two gray Samsonite suitcases – the kind you can drive a truck over.

ANDY

Dough-Boy probably told you I don't carry any Saturday Night Specials or crap like that. It's all out of state, clean, brand new, top-of-the-line stuff.

He places the suitcases on the white bedspread. The suitcases are equipped with special locks, which he quickly opens. Stacked in gray packing foam are rows and rows of brand-new handguns.

TRAVIS

You got a .44 Magnum?

ANDY

That's an expensive gun.

TRAVIS

I got money.

Andy unzips a cowhide leather pouch to reveal a .44 Magnum pistol. He holds it gingerly, as if it were a precious treasure. He opens the chambers and cradles the long eight-inch barrel in his palm. The .44 is a huge, oversized, inhuman gun.

ANDY
(*admiringly*)

It's a monster. Can stop a car – put a bullet right into the block. A premium high resale gun. $350 – that's only a hundred over list.

Easy Andy is a later version of the fast-talking, good-looking kid in

*college who was always making money on one scheme or another. In
high school he sold lottery tickets, in college he scored dope, and now
he's hustling handguns.*

*He holds the Magnum out for Travis's inspection. There's a worship-
ful close-up of the .44 Magnum. It is a monster.*

*Travis hefts the huge gun. It seems out of place in his hand. It is
built on Michelangelo's scale. The Magnum belongs in the hand of a
marble god, not a slight taxi driver. Travis hands the gun back to
Andy.*

> I could sell this gun in Harlem for $500 today – but I just
> deal high-quality goods to high-quality people.
>> (*pause*)
> Now this may be a little big for practical use, in which
> case I'd recommend the .38 Smith and Wesson Special.
> Fine solid gun – nickel-plated. Snub-nosed, otherwise the
> same as the service revolver. Now that'll stop anything
> that moves and it's handy, flexible. The Magnum, you
> know, that's only if you want to splatter it against the wall.
> The movies have driven up the price of the Magnum any-
> way. Everybody wants them now. But the Wesson .38 –
> only $250 – and worth every dime of it.
>> (*hefts .38*)
> Throw in a holster for $10.

Travis hefts the nickel-plated .38, points it out the window.

> Some of these guns are like toys, but a Smith and Wesson,
> man, you can hit somebody over the head with it and it
> will still come back dead on. Nothing beats quality.
>> (*pause*)
> You interested in an automatic?

TRAVIS
I want a .32. Revolver. And a palm gun. That .22 there.

ANDY
That's the Colt .25 – a fine little gun. Don't do a lotta
damage, but it's as fast as the Devil. Handy little gun, you

can carry it almost anywhere. I'll throw it in for another
$125.

*Travis holds the .32 revolver, hefts it, slips it under his belt, and pulls
his shirt over it. He turns from side to side, to see how it rides in his
waist.*

                    TRAVIS
How much for everything?

                    ANDY
The .32's $150 – and you're really getting a good deal now
– and all together it comes to, ah, seven eighty-five for four
pieces and a holster. Hell, I'll give you the holster, we'll
make it seven seventy-five and you've got a deal – a good
one.

                    TRAVIS
How much to get a permit to carry?

                    ANDY
Well, you're talking big money now. I'd say at least five
grand, maybe more, and it would take a while to check it
out. The way things are going now $5,000 is probably low.
You see, I try not to fool with the small-time crap. Too
risky, too little bread. Say six Gs, but if I get the permit
it'll be as solid as the Empire State Building.

                    TRAVIS
Nah, this'll be fine.

                    ANDY
You can't carry in a cab even with a permit – so why
bother?

                    TRAVIS
Is there a firing range around?

                    ANDY
Sure, here, take this card. Go to this place and give 'em
the card. They'll charge you, but there won't be any hassle.

Travis pulls out a roll of crisp one-hundred-dollar bills and counts off eight.

You in 'Nam? Can't help but notice your jacket?

> TRAVIS
> (*looking up*)

Huh?

> ANDY

Vietnam? I saw it on your jacket. Where were you? Bet you got to handle a lot of weapons out there.

Travis hands Andy the bills. Andy counts them and gives Travis a twenty and a five.

> TRAVIS

Yeah. I was all around. One hospital, then the next.

> ANDY
> (*as he counts*)

It's hell out there all right. A real shit-eatin' war. I'll say this, though: it's bringing back a lot of fantastic guns. The market's flooded. Colt automatics are all over.

Pockets the money.

> TRAVIS
> (*intensely*)

They'd never get me to go back. They'd have to shoot me first.
> (*pause*)
You got anything to carry these in?

He gestures to the pistols.

Travis is like a light-switch: for long periods he goes along dark and silent, saying nothing; then suddenly, the current is turned on and the air is filled with the electricity of his personality. Travis's inner intensity sets Andy back a bit, but he quickly recovers.

> ANDY

Sure.

Andy pulls a gym bag from under the bed. He wraps the guns in the sheet in the bag and zips it up. An identical gym bag can be partially seen under the bed. He hands Travis the bag.

You like ball games?

TRAVIS

Huh?

ANDY

I can get you front and center. What do you like? I can get you Mets, Yankees, Knicks, Rangers? Hell, I can get you the Mayor's box.

TRAVIS

Nah. I ain't interested.

Andy closes and locks the suitcases.

ANDY

OK, OK.

Travis turns to leave.

Wait a second, Travis. I'll walk you out.

TRAVIS GETS ORGANIZED

Several weeks later. The face of Travis's apartment has changed. The long, blank wall behind the table is now covered with tacked-up charts, pictures, newspaper clippings, maps. The camera does not come close enough to discern the exact contents of these clippings.

Close-up of Travis in the middle of the floor doing push-ups. He is bareback, wearing only his jeans. There is a long scar across his left side.

TRAVIS (V.O.)

May 29, 1972. I must get in shape. Too much sitting has ruined my body. Twenty-five push-ups each morning, one hundred sit-ups, one hundred knee-bends. I have quit smoking.

Travis still bareback, passes his stiff arm through the flame of a gas burner without flinching a muscle.

Total organization is necessary. Every muscle must be tight.

At the firing range. The cracking sound of rapid-fire pistol shots fills the musty air of the firing range. The walls are heavily sound-proofed, and sawdust is spread over the floor.

Travis stands rock solid, firing the .44 Magnum at an arm's length. With each blasting discharge from the Magnum, Travis's body shudders and shakes, his arm rippling back. Travis quickly bolts himself upright, as if each recoil from the giant gun was a direct attack on his masculinity.

He fires the Magnum as quickly as he can re-set, re-aim, and re-fire. The Magnum empty, he sets it down, picks up the .38 Special, and begins firing as soon as he can aim. After the .38 comes the .25: it is as if he were in a contest to see how quickly he can fire the pistols. After all the guns are discharged, he begins reloading them without a moment's hesitation.

Downrange, the red and white targets have the black outline of a human figure drawn over them. The contour-man convulses under the steady barrage of Travis's rapid-fire shots.

Inside the apartment. Travis, now wearing an unfastened green plaid western shirt, sits at the table writing in his diary. The vial of Bennies rests on the table.

My body fights me always. It won't work, it won't sleep, it won't shit, it won't eat.

Later. Travis, his shirt still open revealing his bare chest, sits on his straight-backed chair watching the TV. The .44 Magnum rests on his lap.

The TV is broadcasting Rock Time, *a late-afternoon local teenage dance and rock show. On screen young teenyboppers are dancing, and the TV cameraman, as any devotee of the genre knows, is relentlessly zooming in on their firm young breasts, fannies, and crotches – a sensibility which reflects Travis's own. These supper-hour rock dance shows are the most unabashedly voyeuristic form of broadcasting the medium has yet developed.*

The hard-rock number ends, and the TV camera cuts to the local disc jockey, a hirsute plastic-looking man of about thirty-five. Five scrumptious teenyboppers are literally hanging on his shoulders and arms, their faces turned up to him in droolish awe. Out of his mouth comes an incessant stream of disc-jockey blather. He is the complete asshole.

TV DISC JOCKEY
Freshingly, fantastic, freaked-out dance time. Can you dig it? Dig on it. You got it, flaunt it.

Travis watches the show, his face hard and unmoving. He is, as the Scriptures would say, pondering all these things in his heart. Why is it the assholes get all the beautiful young chicks? He takes a swig of peach brandy.

THE $20 RIDE

Early evening, about 6.30 p.m. Travis's taxi, with 'Off Duty' light on, sits near the curb somewhere in midtown Manhattan.

Travis runs his hand down the left side of his jacket, attempting to smooth out the bulge in it.

He opens his jacket partially, checking underneath. There rests the nickel-plated .38 Special in its holster.

From his point of view down the street where Travis's taxi is parked: several blocks ahead the red, white, and blue Palantine campaign headquarters are visible.

Travis's eyes resume their watch.

He starts the cab and drives toward the Palantine headquarters.

Tracking point-of-view shot of row of storefronts leading up to Palantine headquarters. Passes headquarters: it is half-empty. A few stalwart supporters continue to work toward the rear of the office. Betsy's desk is vacant.

Sign in window reads: 'ONLY 4 MORE DAYS UNTIL ARRIVAL OF CHARLES PALANTINE.'

Travis's 'Off Duty' light goes off as he speeds up and heads toward a prospective fare.

Later that night, about 9.30. Uptown – 128th and Amsterdam: 'The Jungle.' Travis's taxi pulls up to an address, lets off young black man.

Travis receives fare and tip, takes off.

Travis's point-of-view as he works his way through Harlem back down Seventh Avenue. Cluster of young black street punks pretends to hail cab – we ignore them. One throws wine bottle which crashes in our path – taxi swerves to avoid it.

Camera tracks through sidewalk crowds with the roving, suspicious, antagonistic eye of a taxi driver.

Later that night, about 12.30. Travis is on the Lower East Side, somewhere on B Street, east of Tompkins Square.

The sidewalks are populated with the remains of what was once the hippie movement: teenage street-walkers, junkies, thugs, emaciated loners on the prowl.

Travis's taxi pulls over, letting out a passenger.

Travis pockets his fare, but the rear right door doesn't slam – instead there is the sound of another person jumping into the cab. Travis checks the back seat in the rear-view mirror: there sits a pale hippie prostitute.

The girl is, at best, fourteen or fifteen, although she has been made up to look older. She wears floppy, Janis Joplin-style clothes. Her face is pallid. She wears large blue-tinted sunglasses and multi-colored leg stockings. Her name, as we shall learn later, is Iris. Travis hesitates, looking at her in the mirror.

IRIS
Come on, mister, let's get outta here – quick.

Travis moves to activate the meter, when the rear door opens. Iris is helped out of the cab by a man Travis cannot see.

SPORT
(*to Iris*)
Come on, baby, let's go. This is all a real drag.

Iris lets herself be taken out of the cab. The rear door closes. Sport leans partially in the front window, throwing something on the front seat. Travis looks: it is a crumpled twenty-dollar bill.

Just forget all about this, cabbie. It's nothing.

Travis cannot see the Sport's face completely, but notices he is wearing a lime-green jacket. The voice is that of a man in his early twenties.

Travis turns to catch a glimpse of Sport as he walks off with Iris.

Travis shrugs and turns around. His taxi pulls away.

FOREPLAY TO GUNPLAY

Early morning, 6.00 a.m. Quitting-time – Travis pulls into taxi garage.

Travis pulls into his stall.

He sits in the driver's seat, thinking a moment. He looks to his right: the crumpled twenty-dollar bill still lies there, untouched since it was thrown there six hours previously.

Travis reluctantly picks it up and stuffs it into his jacket pocket as he gets out of the cab. He gathers up his time report and heads toward book-in table.

A short while later, Travis is walking down the sidewalk near the taxi garage. His hands are in his jacket pockets, obscuring the slight bulge on his left side.

He turns into the box-office of the porno theater. He reaches into jacket pocket for money to purchase ticket and pulls out crumpled twenty-dollar bill. He decides not to use it and pays for ticket out of his wallet instead.

Travis walks past the concession stand en route to the darkened theater auditorium. A young man is now sitting listlessly behind the concessions counter.

Inside the porno theater auditorium Travis slouches down into his seat, his face glowing in the reflected light from the screen.

> FEMALE MOVIE VOICE (O.S.)
> Oh, come on, now, down, lick it, come on . . . Mmm, that's good. Ahh, ahh, more . . .

Travis averts his eyes as the action on screen becomes too graphic. Placing his stiffened right hand beside his eyes, Travis can, by turning it inward, shut off or open up his field of vision by small degrees.

Movie voice diminishes, replaced by sound of Travis's voice-over.

> TRAVIS (V.O.)
> The idea has been growing in my brain . . .

Tracking shot to wall of Travis's apartment. Camera moves slowly across wall covered with clippings, notes, maps, pictures. We now see their contents clearly:

The wall is covered with Charles Palantine political paraphernalia; there are pictures of him, newspaper articles, leaflets, bumper stickers. As the camera moves along it discovers a sketch of Plaza Hotel, Kennedy Airport, and cut-up sections of city maps with notations written in. There is a lengthy New York Times *clipping detailing the increased Secret Security Protection during the primaries. A section pertaining to Palantine is underlined. Further along there is a sheet reading 'traveling schedule' and a calendar for June with finely written notations written over the dates.*

> . . . for some time. True Force. All the king's men cannot put it back together again.

As the camera reaches the end of its track, it finds Travis, standing, his shirt open, by the mattress. He is wearing the empty holster, and the .44 is in his hand.

In the shots that follow Travis gives the audience a lesson in gunmanship.

He practices fast-drawing the .38 Special from his holster and firing it.

He hooks the .44 into his pants behind his back and practices withdrawing it. He holds the .44 firmly at an arm's length, tightening his forearm muscles.

He has worked out a system of metal gliders taped to his inner forearm, whereby the Colt .25 can rest hidden behind the upper forearm until a spring near the elbow is activated, sending the .25 flying down the gliders into his palm. He has cut open his shirt to accommodate the gun mechanism and now checks in the mirror to see how well the gun is hidden.

He straps an Army combat knife to his calf and cuts a slit in his jeans where the knife can be pulled out quickly.

He now tries on various combinations of shirts, sweaters, and jackets in front of the mirror to see how well he can hide all the handguns he wishes to carry. Finally, wearing two western shirts, a sweater, and jacket, he manages to obscure the location of all three guns, although he resembles a hunter bundled up against the Arctic winter.

He sits at the table dum-dumming the .44 bullets – cutting 'x's across the bullet heads.

From his point of view he scans the objects of his room through the scope of the .38.

Travis stands in the middle of his apartment, staring at his Palantine wall. His eyes are glazed with introspection; he sees nothing but himself.

> Listen, you screwheads: Here is a man . . .

Travis lies on his mattress, all bundled up in his shirts, sweater, jacket, and guns. His face is turned toward the ceiling, but his eyes are closed. Although the room is flooded with light, he is finally catching some sleep. The big furry animal drifts into his own world.

> . . . who wouldn't take it any more, a man who stood up against the scum, the cunts, the dogs, the filth. Here is . . .

Voice trails off.

Close-up of diary: entry ends 'Here is' followed by erratic series of dots.

INCIDENT IN A DELI

Night: the taxis are roaming the slick streets.

Some time after 2.00 a.m., Travis pulls his cab to the curb near an all-night delicatessen in Spanish Harlem. The streets are relatively deserted.

Travis waves to storekeeper as he walks past counter.

                    TRAVIS
     Hey, Melio.

Spanish rhythm-and-blues blares from a cheap radio. Travis walks over to dairy counter in rear of the store, picks out a pint of chocolate milk, goes over to the open cooler and picks through various chilled prepackaged sandwiches. He overhears a voice as he looks at the sandwiches.

When Travis returns to the counter with the chocolate milk and a sandwich in one hand, he sees a young black man holding a gun on Melio. The stick-up man is nervous, hopped-up, or both: he bounces on the balls of his cheap, worn black tennis shoes – a strung-out junkie on a desperation ride. The stick-up man, a thorough unprofessional, doesn't notice Travis.

Melio watches the stick-up man closely, deciding what to do himself.

                  STICK-UP MAN
                  (*shaking gun*)
     Come on, man. Quick, quick, quick – let's see that bread.

It doesn't take Travis long to decide what to do: without hesitation he pulls his .32 from his jacket pocket.

                    TRAVIS
     Hey, dude!

Stick-up man, surprised, turns toward Travis, finding only an exploding .32. The stick-up man's lower jaw bursts open with blood as he reels and crashes to the floor. There is no emotion on Travis's face.

As the stick-up man falls, Melio leans over the counter, wielding his battered .38. He is about to fire when he realizes the man is already dead.

Melio, charged up, turns his gun toward Travis, then, realizing the danger is over, lowers it again.

MELIO

Thanks, man. Figured I'd get him on the way out.

Travis sets his .32 on the counter.

TRAVIS

You're gonna have to cover me on this one, Melio. I can't stay for the cop show.

MELIO

You can't do that, Travis. You're my witness.

TRAVIS

The hell I can't. It's no sweat for you. What is this for you, number five?

Melio smiles and holds up four fingers.

MELIO

No, only four.
(*shrugs*)
All right, Travis, I'll do what I can.

TRAVIS

Thanks a lot.

He exits. Melio picks up the phone and starts dialing. The bloody body lies on the floor unmoving.

Travis, still carrying his pint of chocolate milk and sandwich, walks down the empty sidewalk and enters his cab. The street is deserted.

MID-AFTERNOON MELODRAMA

Direct cut to pornographic movie: this is the first time we have actually seen the porno movie itself. Several actors and actresses are dallying on screen in whatever manner the ratings board deems permissible.

Whatever the action, the movie's decor is strictly Zody's – ersatz landscape paintings, tufted bedspreads. As in most porno films, the actors look up occasionally toward the camera to receive instructions. Studio grunts, groans, and moans of pleasure have been dubbed in.

Action on screen begins to go into slow motion, the actors and actresses gradually transforming obscenity into poetry.

Cut to Travis, sitting in his chair in his apartment, watching afternoon soap opera. He is cleaning his .38 and eating from a jar of apple sauce. Soap-opera audio continues.

He watches the soap opera without expression.

Soundtrack of film also slows down, gradually mixing with and then becoming the soundtrack of a mid-afternoon TV soap opera. A young girl and boy are talking in those familiar soap-opera voices about a third party, the girl's mother, who had tried to terminate their 'relationship.'

Cut to television: The boy is visiting the girl in her hospital room. Both look as if they've stepped out of the Blue Chip Stamp catalogue.

> SOAP OPERA BOY
> Is it that she just doesn't – like me?

> SOAP OPERA GIRL
> (*hesitantly*)
> Well, Jim, it's just that – I don't know how to say this – it's that she thinks your parents aren't . . . good enough, I guess.

Travis, through cleaning his gun, begins to play a game with the television set.

He places the heel of his boot at the top of the melon crate which supports the TV. Then, slowly rocking his heel back and forth, he sees how far he can tip the melon crate without knocking it over.

The TV, still broadcasting the hospital-room melodrama, rocks back and forth.

Travis pushes the TV further and further until finally the inevitable happens – the crate tips backwards, sending the portable TV crashing to the floor.

There is a short flash and the TV screen turns white. Travis, realizing what he has done, bends over, turns the TV upright on the floor, fiddles with the knobs, slaps it, and tries to reactivate the vanished image. Travis's efforts are futile; a tube has broken, and the TV will not come back to life.

TRAVIS
(*to himself*)

Damn, damn.

He bends over in the chair and places his head in his hands, despairing of himself.

THE WIZARD SPEAKS

At about 1 a.m. Travis pulls his cab behind a line of empty taxis parked outside the Bellmore Cafeteria, a cabbie hangout on Park Avenue South.

He locks his cab and walks past the line of taxis. He sidesteps past two drunken fighting bums and enters the Bellmore.

A loud buzzer rings as Travis steps into the Bellmore. He pulls a ticket from the dispenser (silencing the buzzer) and walks toward the wall-length counter. An assortment of cabbies are seated around a formica-topped table near the rear of the cafeteria. Some are barely awake, some are eating, the rest are swapping stories and small talk.

Wizard, Dough-Boy, Charlie T, and a fourth cabbie are seated at a long table.

WIZARD

You know Eddie, he's the new hippie kid in our group, long hair . . .

Wizard demonstrates length of hair and others nod.

. . . he called up the Dispatcher last night. Charlie McCall, our dispatcher . . .

DOUGH-BOY

One-Ball McCall?

WIZARD

That's the guy. Eddie calls him up and says, 'Hey, what do you want me to do? I'm over here at Poly Prep. I got a girl in the back and she doesn't have the fare. She wants me to come in back and collect. What should I do?'

The cabbies laugh. Across the cafeteria Travis selects a cup of coffee and some pastries.

CHARLIE T

This is on the two-way with about a hundred and fifty cats listenin' in.

WIZARD

McCall says, 'How much on the meter?' Eddie comes back and says, 'Two-fifty.' McCall says, 'Is she worth it?'

More laughter.

DOUGH-BOY

Fuckin' One-Ball.

WIZARD

And the kid says, 'Yeah. She's about nineteen, good-lookin'.' McCall says, 'What can I tell you?'

FOURTH CABBIE

Should have told him to get an OK from the front office.

WIZARD

McCall says, 'Well, if you want some help I'll see if I can send some units out.'

CHARLIE T

Yeah. About a hundred and fifty.

DOUGH-BOY

I hope he had a checker.

WIZARD

She was just a kid. Stoned, you know.

*Travis, carrying his coffee and pastries, walks over to their table.
Charlie T spots him.*

CHARLIE T

Hiya, Killer.

*Charlie forms his hand into a pistol, cocks and fires, making the
sound 'Pgghew.' Travis nods.*

WIZARD

You're getting a rep, Travis.

Travis sits down and the other cabbies resume their conversation.

CHARLIE T

Got the five you owe me, Killer?

*Travis reaches into his pocket and pulls out a roll of small denomi-
nation bills. The crumpled $20 bill falls on to the table. Travis stares
at it a moment. He unfolds a five, gives it to Charlie T, then picks up
the crumpled $20 and puts it back into his jacket pocket.*

WIZARD
(*out of shot, to Travis*)

What's the action around?

TRAVIS

Slow.

CHARLIE T

Shit yes. Night would'a been dead if I hadn't grabbed an
outta towner at Kennedy. Took him round the horn and
got a five-dollar tip to boot.

WIZARD
(*joking*)

One of these days we're gonna turn you in, Charlie T.
Fleecin' the hicks like that.

DOUGH-BOY

Remember the time this cat picks up four dudes from the
other side, Pakistanis I think they were, holds up their
passports to the toll-booth collector on the bridge and

charges 'em ten bucks each for crossing the border?

They all laugh.

> CHARLIE T
>
> Hell, I know'd you to do worse.

> DOUGH-BOY
>
> Least I'm no airport rat. I work the whole town.

> CHARLIE T
> (*chuckling*)
>
> It's a living.

Wizard gets up to leave.

> WIZARD
>
> Well, I'm shovin' on.

He nods and walks toward the cashier. After a second's thought, Travis calls to him:

> TRAVIS
>
> Hey, Wiz, just a second. I wanna talk to you.

Wizard waits for Travis as he takes a final gulp of coffee and catches up with him. Charlie T calls to Travis as they go:

> CHARLIE T
>
> See ya, Killer. Don't forget your pea shooter.

Charlie T cocks his imaginary gun again, fires, and chuckles. Wizard and Travis nod goodbye, pay the cashier, and exit. Travis follows Wizard out on to the sidewalk. He follows him as he walks toward his cab. He has something on his mind, something he wants to talk to Wizard about.

> TRAVIS
> (*as they walk*)
>
> Hey, Wiz.

> WIZARD
>
> Yeah?

Wizard leans back against his cab. Travis is about to speak when he spots a group of black and Puerto Rican street punks, aged between twelve and fifteen, jiving down the sidewalk toward him. One tosses a spray-paint can around his back, basketball style. Another mocks as if he's going to scratch a key along one of the cabs.

Wizard has no visible reaction. A flash of controlled anger crosses Travis's face. He stares at the boy with the poised key. It is the same look that crossed his face in the Harlem deli. We are reminded with a jolt that the killer lies just beneath Travis's surface.

The black punk must instinctively realize this too, because he makes a cocky show of putting the key back into his pocket and be-bopping around Travis and Wizard.

The young mean-streeters continue down the street and Travis turns back to Wizard.

Across the street, in the background, a junkie huddles in a doorway.

> TRAVIS
> (*hesitant*)

Wiz?

> WIZARD

Yeah?

> TRAVIS

Look, ah, we never talked much, you and me . . .

> WIZARD

Yeah?

> TRAVIS

I wanted to ask you something, on account you've been around so long.

> WIZARD

Shoot. They don't call me the Wizard for nothing.

> TRAVIS

Well, I just, you know . . .

> WIZARD

Things got ya down?

TRAVIS

Real down.

WIZARD

It happens.

TRAVIS

Sometimes it gets so I just don't know what I'm gonna do.
I get some real crazy ideas, you know? Just go out and do
somethin'.

WIZARD

The taxi life, you mean.

TRAVIS

Yeah.

WIZARD
(*nods*)

I know.

TRAVIS

Like do *anything*, you know.

WIZARD

Travis, look, I dig it. Let me explain. You choose a certain
way of life. You live it. It becomes what you are. I've been
a hack twenty-seven years, the last ten at night. Still don't
own my own cab. I guess that's the way I want it. You see,
that must be what I am.

*A police car stops across the street. Two patrolmen get out and roust
the junkie from his doorway.*

Look, a person does a certain thing and that's all there is
to it. It becomes what he is. Why fight it? What do you
know? How long you been a hack, a couple months?
You're like a peg and you get dropped into a slot and you
got to squirm and wiggle around a while until you fit in.

TRAVIS
(*pause*)

That's just about the dumbest thing I ever heard, Wizard.

WIZARD

What do you expect, Bertrand Russell? I've been a cabbie
all my life, what do I know?

(*pauses*)

I don't even know what you're talking about.

TRAVIS

Neither do I, I guess.

WIZARD

You fit in. It's lonely, it's rough at first. But you fit in. You
got no choice.

TRAVIS

Yeah. Sorry, Wizard?

WIZARD

Don't worry, Killer. You'll be all right.

(*pauses*)

I seen enough to know.

TRAVIS

Thanks.

*Wizard gives Travis a short wave implying, 'Chin up, old boy,' and
walks around to the driver's side of his cab. He drives off, leaving
the street to its natural inhabitants.*

A NEW FACE IN THE CROWD

Outside, at the Charles Palantine rally. Day.

*A rally platform in a supermarket parking lot somewhere in Queens
is draped in red, white, and blue bunting.*

*A crowd about 500 strong mills about, waiting for the rally to begin.
Piped pop-country music plays over the loudspeaker system. A cadre
of secret service men, with their distinctive metallic gray suits, sun
glasses, and football physiques, stands out in the crowd. On the platform are seated an assortment of local politicos as well as some
Palantine workers and advisers.*

Tom is silently reading something on the podium, and Betsy stands on the platform steps talking to another worker.

Tom looks up and to his left for a moment, then returns to what he was reading. Then he returns his gaze to the upper left, watching something very closely.

After a moment he walks over to the steps where Betsy is standing.

TOM

Betsy, come over here a moment.

BETSY

What is it? I'm busy.

TOM
(*insistent*)

Just follow me.

Betsy excuses herself and walks across the platform with Tom. As they stand to the rear of the platform, Tom secretively makes a gesture with his eyes and says out of the side of his mouth:

Look there.

Her eyes follow his.

No, over further – get your glasses – yes, over there. Isn't that little guy the same guy that was bugging you around the office about a month ago?

Betsy, putting on her glasses, looks closely. She tries not to make her stare too obvious.

BETSY

No, I don't think so.
(*a pause*)

That's someone else.

TOM

Now look more closely. Look around the eyes and chin. See? See there?

Camera closes in on Travis standing in the crowd: he has shaved his head to a short stubble. There he is: brush-cut, wearing a giant grin and a large 'Palantine '72' button. Although it is a pleasant sunny day, Travis is wearing a bulky bulged-out Army jacket.

Travis looks warily from side to side and vanishes in the crowd.

A short while later, Travis walks up to a secret service man standing near the fringes of the crowd. The secret service man – in sunglasses, gray suit, ever-roving eyes – is immediately identifiable.

Whenever Travis confronts a symbol of authority, he becomes like a young boy. This time is no exception, although one suspects there is a plan hatching beneath the boyish exterior. The secret service man, for his part, is about as talkative as the Sphinx.

> TRAVIS
> Are you a secret service man?

> SECRET SERVICE MAN
> (*indifferently*)
> Why do you ask?

> TRAVIS
> I've seen a lot of suspicious-looking people around here today.

Secret service man glances at Travis momentarily.

> SECRET SERVICE MAN
> Who?

> TRAVIS
> Oh, lots. I don't know where they all are now. There used to be one standing over there.

He points.

The secret service man's gaze follows Travis's finger for a second, then returns to Travis.

> Is it hard to get to be a secret service man?

> SECRET SERVICE MAN
> Why?

TRAVIS

I kinda thought I might make a good one. I'm very observant.

SECRET SERVICE MAN

Oh?

TRAVIS

I was in the Army too.
(*a pause*)
And I'm good with crowds.

The secret service man is starting to get interested in Travis: he definitely ranks as a suspicious character.

SECRET SERVICE MAN

Is that so?

TRAVIS

What kind of guns do you guys use? .38s?

The secret service man decides it's time to get some more information on Travis:

SECRET SERVICE MAN

Look, um, if you give me your name and address, we'll send you the information on how to apply.

TRAVIS

You would, huh?

SECRET SERVICE MAN
(*taking out notepad*)

Sure.

TRAVIS

My name is Henry Krinkle – that's with a K. K-R-I-N-K-L-E. I live at 13 1/2 Hopper Avenue, Fair Lawn, New Jersey. Zip code 07410.
(*a pause*)
Got that?

SECRET SERVICE MAN
Sure, Henry. I got it all. We'll send you all the stuff all
right.

TRAVIS
Great, hey. Thanks a lot.

*The secret service man motions to a secret service photographer to
catch a picture of Travis. Travis notices this, and quickly slips away
into the crowd.*

*Travis sits at his desk in his apartment, writing. He wears jeans,
western shirt, and empty holster.*

TRAVIS (V.O.)
June 11. Eight rallies in six more days. The time is coming.

A REMEMBERED FACE

*Night. Travis's taxi picks up a fare in the midtown area and heads
downtown.*

*Lower East Side. Travis lets off fare on B Street and cuts across
toward Tompkins Square.*

Travis turns the corner when skreetch! *he suddenly hits the brakes,
causing the cab to rock back and forth.*

*He has almost hit a young girl recklessly crossing the street. She
thumps her hand on the taxi hood to regain her balance and stares
in shock through the front window. Close-up of girl's face.*

*Travis recognizes her face: it's Iris, the girl in his taxi a week or so
before. Iris looks at Travis sharply, then turns and continues walking.*

*Travis's eyes follow her and she rejoins a girlfriend. They are both
dressed as hippie hookers: sloppy clothes, boots, jeans, floppy hats.
And the old come-hither walk is unmistakable.*

*Travis follows Iris and her girlfriend slowly as they walk down the
sidewalk.*

Travis's point of view: he examines them from bottom to top — boots, legs, thighs, breasts, faces, hats.

As Travis rolls astride the girls, he notices the familiar fringe of a suede jacket standing in the shadows. The girls look toward the shadowed figure, smile, acknowledge some unheard comment, and continue on.

Iris looks back uneasily at Travis's taxi and continues on. On the corner stand two well-to-do college students, somewhat out of place in this environment, but making every attempt to groove on it. They are high on something or other.

The girls spot the college students and walk over to them. They exchange some small talk and walk off together. There is little subtlety involved: it is obviously a pick-up.

Travis must negotiate a turn around the corner if he is to continue following the girls and their collegiate johns. This is not so easy, since the traffic is heavy.

As Travis slows down to make the turn, he notices another hippie hooker who had been watching him watching Iris and her girlfriend. She walks over to the taxi, leans in the open left front window and gives Travis the come-on disguised as an innocent question:

HIPPIE HOOKER
(*close-up*)

Hey, cabbie! You comin' or goin'?

Travis quickly turns his face away from her in a combination of shock, embarrassment, and revulsion. He is the child caught with his hand in the cookie jar. The very presence of this crassly, openly sexual human being frightens and sickens him. He takes off with a screech. His taxi shoots down the block.

CAMPAIGN PROMISES

A hot June day. Travis's taxi, the 'Off Duty' sign on, is parked against the curb somewhere in Harlem. White cops, secret service men, and reporters punctuate the otherwise black crowds walking to and fro in the background.

Charles Palantine's voice can be heard coming from a distant loud-speaker system. It is a political rally.

Travis sits behind the wheel, coldly staring at something in the distance. His hair, of course, is still clipped short and he wears mirror-reflecting sunglasses. Even though a drop of sweat is working its way down his cheek, Travis wears his Army jacket with the bulge on the left side – the .38 Smith and Wesson bulge.

A block away, Palantine stands on a platform outside his uptown campaign headquarters. On the platform sit an array of black digni-taries. Near by we recognize the secret service man who Travis spoke to at the earlier rally: he scans the crowd anxiously. Palantine is speaking animatedly. He is an excellent speaker and captures the attention. He drives hard toward his arguments, crashes down on his points. His strained voice rings with sincerity and anger. Close-up of Palantine as he speaks. He is dressed in rolled-up shirtsleeves and sweat pours down his face.

PALANTINE

The time has come to put an end to the things that divide us: racism, poverty, war – and to those persons who seek to divide us. Never have I seen such a group of high offi-cials from the President to Senate leaders to Cabinet members . . .

Cut to Travis: no expression. Palantine's words are barely distin-guishable from a block away.

In distance.

. . . pit black against white, young against old, sew anger, disunity and suspicion – and all in the name of the 'good of the country.' Well, their game is over.

Applause.

All their names are over. Now is the time to stand up against such foolishness, propaganda, and demagoguery. Now is the time for one man to stand up and accept his neighbor, for one man to give in order that all might receive. Is unity and love of common good such a lost thing?

All live sound ceases as Travis's narration begins. He is reading from a letter or card he has just written.

As he speaks we see shots of Palantine speaking, a seated row of young black Palantine red, white, and blue bedecked cheerleaders, secret service agents examining the crowd, and so forth. These shots have no direct relationship to the narration.

> TRAVIS (V.O.)
> (*reading*)

'Dear Father and Mother,
June is the month, I remember, which brings not only your wedding anniversary, but also Father's Day and Mother's birthday. I'm sorry I can't remember the exact dates, but I hope this card will take care of all of them.

   I'm sorry I again cannot send you my address like I promised to last year, but the sensitive nature of my work for the Army demands utmost secrecy. I know you will understand.

   I am healthy and well and making lots of money. I have been going with a girl for several months and I know you would be proud if you could see her. Her name is Betsy, but I can tell you no more than that –'

As Travis reads the third paragraph, a policeman is seen walking from behind Travis's taxi to his window. The policeman's voice comes during a pause in the narration. Live sound resumes.

> POLICEMAN
> (*standing near window*)

Hey, cabbie, you can't park here.

> TRAVIS
> (*penitent*)

Sorry, officer.

> POLICEMAN

You waiting for a fare?

Policeman leans his head in window, inspecting the cab. As he does,

Travis slides his right hand into the left side of his jacket, ready to draw his revolver.

TRAVIS

No, officer.

POLICEMAN

All right, move it.

Travis starts up his taxi and drives off.

Live sound again ceases as Travis resumes reading letter as taxi drives away.

As Travis reads the final paragraph, scene cuts to inside his apartment where Travis sits at his table.

TRAVIS (V.O.)
(resuming reading)

'I hope this card finds you all well, as it does me. I hope no one has died. Don't worry about me. One day there will be a knock on the door and it will be me.
Love, Travis.'

Travis, at his desk, examines the card upon which he has just written this letter.

Close-up cover of card. It is a 25¢ wedding anniversary card with a four-color embossed cover. The design could only be described as kitsch. A cartoon Mr and Mrs All-America stand before an outdoor barbecuing grill, clicking salt and pepper shakers in a toast. Sentiment reads:

HAPPY ANNIVERSARY
To a Couple
Who Have Found
the Perfect Combination
For Marriage . . .

The card opens to read:

LOVE!

Underneath the word 'Love!' begins Travis's short message to his parents, a message which extends to the back cover of the card.

SWEET IRIS

Night on the Lower East Side. Travis sits parked in the dark shadows of a side street. The lone wolf waits.

He watches the slum goddesses as they work the section of the street reserved for hippie hookers.

Travis's point of view: some of the young street girls are arrogant, almost aggressive, others are more insecure and inexperienced. A black man charges down the sidewalk across the street from Travis. He walks at a fast, maniacal clip, looking only at the sidewalk in front of him. Out of his mouth comes a continuous stream of invective: 'That-cock-sucking-crazy-no-good-asshole-bitch-when-I-get-my-fucking-fingers-on-her-nigger-tits-I'm-gonna-ring-'em-and-shit-up-her ass . . .' and so on. He is out of control. Nobody seems to notice or care.

Travis takes a swig of peach brandy and continues his stake-out. Finally, he spies the object of his search: Iris walks down the sidewalk with her girlfriend. She wears her large blue sunglasses. Travis checks to see if his .38 is in place (it is), opens the door, and exits from the cab.

Flipping up the collar of his Army jacket, Travis slouches over and walks toward Iris. He sidles up next to her and walks beside her: Travis always looks most suspicious when he's trying to appear innocent.

TRAVIS
(*shy*)

Hello.

IRIS

You looking for some action?

TRAVIS

Well . . . I guess so.

IRIS
(*eyeing him*)

All right.

(*a pause*)

You see that guy over there?

(*nods*)

His name is Sport. Go talk to him. I'll wait here.

Travis's eyes follow Iris's nod until they reach Sport, standing in a doorway in his lime-green jacket. Travis walks toward him.

Sport, a thirtyish white greaser, has the affectations of a black pimp. His hips are jiving, his fingers softly snapping. He sings to himself, 'Going to the chapel, gonna get married . . .' His complexion is sallow; his eyes cold and venal. He could only seem romantic to a confused under-aged runaway.

TRAVIS

Your name Sport?

Sport immediately takes Travis for an undercover cop. He extends his crossed wrists as if to be handcuffed.

SPORT

Here, officer, take me in. I'm clean. I didn't do it. Got a ticket once in Jersey, that's all. Honest, officer.

TRAVIS

Your name Sport?

SPORT

Anything you say, officer.

TRAVIS

I'm no cop.

(*looks back at Iris*)

I want some action.

SPORT

I saw. $20 fifteen minutes. $30 half hour.

TRAVIS

Shit.

SPORT

Take it or leave it.

TRAVIS

I'll take it.

He digs in his pocket for money.

SPORT

No, not me. There'll be an elderly gent to take the bread.

Travis turns to walk away.

Catch you later, Copper.

Travis freezes, not saying anything. He turns back toward Sport.

TRAVIS

I'm no cop.

SPORT

Well, if you are, it's entrapment already.

TRAVIS

I'm hip.

SPORT

Funny, you don't look hip.

He laughs.

Travis walks back to Iris. She motions for Travis to follow her and he does. They turn the corner and walk about a block, saying nothing. Iris turns into a darkened doorway and Travis follows her.

At the top of the dark stairs Iris and Travis enter a dimly lit hallway. On either side are doors with apartment numbers. Iris turns toward the first door, No. 2.

IRIS

This is my room.

At the far end of the darkened corridor sits a huge old man. His face is obscured by shadow. Travis is about to enter the room when the old man speaks up:

OLD MAN

Hey, cowboy!

Travis turns his head toward the old man, who has stood up and is advancing toward him.

(*motioning to Travis's jacket*)

The rod.

(*a pause*)

Gimme the rod, cowboy.

Travis hesitates a moment, uncertain what to do. The old man reaches in Travis's jacket and pulls out the .38 Special.

This ain't Dodge City, cowboy. You don't need no piece.

(*glances at watch*)

I'm keepin' time.

Travis enters No. 2 with Iris.

Travis looks around Iris's room: although dimly lit, the room is brightly decorated. There is an orange shag carpet, deep brown walls, and an old red velvet sofa. On the walls are posters of Mick Jagger, Bob Dylan, and Peter Fonda. A Neil Young album is playing on a small phonograph.

This is where Iris lives: it bears the individual touch of a young girl.

Iris lights a cigarette, takes a single puff and places it in an ashtray on the bedstand.

TRAVIS

Why you hang around with them greasers?

IRIS

A girl needs protection.

TRAVIS

Yeah. From the likes of them.

IRIS

(*shrugs*)

It's your time, mister. Fifteen minutes ain't long.

(*gestures to cigarette*)
That cigarette burns out, your time is up.

Iris sits on the edge of the bed and removes her hat and coat. She takes off her blue-tinted sunglasses – her last defense. Without the paraphernalia of adulthood, Iris looks like the little girl she is. About fourteen, fifteen.

TRAVIS
What's your name?

IRIS
Easy.

TRAVIS
That ain't much of a name.

IRIS
It's easy to remember. Easy Lay.

TRAVIS
What's your real name?

IRIS
I don't like my real name.

TRAVIS
(*insistent*)
What's your real name?

IRIS
Iris.

TRAVIS
That's a nice name.

IRIS
That's what you think.

She unbuttons her shirt, revealing her small pathetic breasts – two young doves hiding from a winter wind. Travis is unnerved by her partial nudity.

TRAVIS

Don't you remember me? Button your shirt.

Iris buttons only the bottom button on her shirt.

IRIS
(*examining him*)

Why? Who are you?

TRAVIS

I drive a taxi. You tried to get away one night. Remember?

IRIS

No.

TRAVIS

You tried to run away in my taxi but your friend – Sport – wouldn't let you.

IRIS

I don't remember.

TRAVIS

It don't matter. I'm gonna get you outta here.

He looks toward door.

IRIS

We better make it, or Sport'll get mad. How do you want to make it?

TRAVIS
(*pressured*)

I don't want to make it. I came here to get you out.

IRIS

You want to make it like this?

She goes for his fly.

Travis pushes her hand away. He sits beside her on the edge of the bed.

TRAVIS
(*taking her by the shoulders*)
Can't you listen to me? Don't you want to get out of here?

IRIS
Why should I want to get out of here? This is where I live.

TRAVIS
(*exasperated*)
But *you're* the one that wanted to get away. *You're* the one
that came into my cab.

IRIS
I must'a been stoned.

TRAVIS
Do they drug you?

IRIS
(*reproving*)
Oh, come off it, man.

*She tries to unzip Travis's fly. This only unnerves Travis more: sex-
ual contact is something he's never really confronted.*

TRAVIS
Listen . . .

IRIS
Don't you want to make it?
(*a pause*)
Can't you make it?

She works on Travis's crotch off camera. He bats her hand away.

TRAVIS
(*distraught*)
I want to *help* you.

*He is getting increasingly panicked, but Iris only thinks this is part
of his particular thing and tries to overcome it.*

                              IRIS
                          (*catching on*)
        You can't make it, can you?
                          (*a pause*)
        I can help you.

*Iris lowers her head to go down on Travis. Travis, seeing this, jumps
up in panic. He stands several feet from Iris. His fly is still open, and
the white of his underwear shows through his jeans. He is starting to
come apart.*

                            TRAVIS
        Fuck it! Fuck it! Fuck it! Fuck it! Fuck it! Fuck it! Fuck it!

                              IRIS
                          (*confused*)
        You can do it in my mouth.

                            TRAVIS
        Don't you understand anything?

*Iris says nothing. After a moment, Travis again sits on the bed beside
Iris. She no longer tries to make him. There is a moment of silence.
Iris puts her arm around his shoulder.*

                              IRIS
        You don't *have* to make it, mister.

Travis rests a moment, collecting himself. Finally, he says:

                            TRAVIS
                          (*slowly*)
        Do you understand why I came here?

                              IRIS
        I think so. I tried to get into your cab one night, and now
        you want to come and take me away.

                            TRAVIS
        Don't you want to go?

                              IRIS
        I can leave any time I want.

TRAVIS

But that one night?

IRIS

I *was* stoned. That's why they stopped me. When I'm not stoned, I got no place else to go. They just protect me from myself.

There is a pause. Travis smiles and shrugs apologetically.

Travis looks at Iris's cigarette. It's burning down to the butt.

TRAVIS

Well, I tried.

IRIS
(*compassionate*)
I understand, mister. It means something, really.

TRAVIS
(*getting up*)
Can I see you again?

IRIS

That's not hard to do.

TRAVIS

No, I mean really. This is nothing for a person to do.

IRIS

Sure. All right. We'll have breakfast. I get up about one o'clock. Tomorrow.

TRAVIS
(*thinking*)
Well tomorrow noon there's a . . . I got a . . .

Iris is interfering with Travis's assassination schedule.

IRIS

Well, you want to or not?

TRAVIS
(*deciding*)

OK. It's a date. I'll see you here, then.

Travis turns; Iris smiles.

Oh, Iris?

IRIS

Yes?

TRAVIS

My name's Travis.

IRIS

Thank you, Travis.

TRAVIS

So long, Iris.
(*a pause*)
Sweet Iris.

He smiles.

Travis exits. He closes the door to No. 2 and stands in the corridor for a moment.

The old man slowly walks from the dark end of the hallway with Travis's .38 in his hand. Old man stands near Travis, and checks his watch.

OLD MAN
(*holding gun*)

I think this is yours, cowboy.

Travis reaches in his jacket pocket and pulls out the familiar crumpled $20 bill. He makes a big show of stuffing the wrinkled bill into the old man's hand. The old man doesn't understand the significance of it.

TRAVIS
(*with restrained anger*)

Here's the twenty bucks, old man. You better damn well spend it right.

He turns and walks away.

                    OLD MAN
            (*as Travis walks downstairs*)
Come back any time you want, cowboy. But without the
rod – please.

Travis does not respond.

St Regis suite. Noon.

*Palantine, Tom, and Palantine's assistant are seated in a garishly
decorated suite.*

                    ASSISTANT
Well, at least it wasn't chicken.

                    PALANTINE
It wasn't? I thought it was. It *tasted* like chicken.

                    TOM
C'mon, Senator. That was a class dinner. The St Regis is a
class joint. That was veal.

                    PALANTINE
Was it? It sure tasted like chicken to me.
                    (*pause*)
Lately, everything tastes like chicken to me.

                    ASSISTANT
Everything? Got to watch your gut.

                    PALANTINE
What about it? I took twenty off before we started this
thing.

                    ASSISTANT
And you've put ten of it back on.

                    PALANTINE
Ten? I don't think so. You really think so? Ten?

TOM

Those TV cameras do. I caught the rally on CBS. You looked a little paunchy.

PALANTINE

I don't think I gained ten pounds.

Palantine gets up and walks over to the window. Its bars form a cross-sight on his head.

(*weary, to himself*)

Jesus Christ.

He looks at the crowded traffic on Fifth Avenue eighteen floors below. It is a mass of yellow.

Fifth Avenue. Noon.

Travis's cab pulls away from the yellow mass and heads downtown.

LATE BREAKFAST

Exterior of downtown coffee shop. Travis's cab is parked near a neighborhood Bickford's.

Travis and Iris are having a late breakfast at a middle-class East Side coffee shop. It is about 1.30 p.m.

Iris is dressed more sensibly, wearing jeans and a maroon sweater. Her face is freshly washed and her hair combed out.

Seen this way, Iris looks no different than any other young girl in the big city. Other patrons of the coffee shop most likely assume she is having lunch with her big brother.

They are both having an all-American breakfast: ham and eggs, large glasses of orange juice, coffee.

Outside her environment, Iris seems the more pathetic. She seems unsure, nervous, unable to hold a subject for more than thirty seconds. Her gestures are too broad, her voice too mannered. We sympathize with Travis's paternal response: this girl is in trouble.

IRIS

. . . and after that Sport and I just started hanging out . . .

TRAVIS

Where is home?

Iris removes her large blue-tinted sunglasses and fishes through her bag for another pair.

IRIS

I got so many sunglasses. I couldn't live without my shades, man. I must have twelve pair of shades.

She finds a pink-tinted pair and puts them on.

TRAVIS

Where?

IRIS

Pittsburgh.

TRAVIS

I ain't ever been there, but it don't seem like such a bad place.

IRIS
(*voice rising*)

Why do you want me to go back to my parents? They hate me. Why do you think I split? There ain't nothin' there.

TRAVIS

But you can't live like this. It's hell. Girls should live at home.

IRIS
(*playfully*)

Didn't you ever hear of women's lib?

There is a short quick silence; Travis's eyes retract.

TRAVIS
(*ignoring her question*)

Young girls are supposed to dress up, go to school, play with boys, you know, that kinda stuff.

Iris places a large gob of jam on her unbuttered toast and folds the bread over like a hotdog.

> IRIS
>
> God, are *you* square.

> TRAVIS
> (*releasing pent-up tension*)
> At least I don't walk the streets like a skunk pussy. I don't screw and fuck with killers and junkies.

Iris motions him to lower his voice.

> IRIS
>
> Who's a killer?

> TRAVIS
>
> That fella 'Sport' looks like a killer to me.

> IRIS
>
> He never killed nobody. He's a Libra.

> TRAVIS
>
> Huh?

> IRIS
>
> I'm a Libra too. That's why we get along so well.

> TRAVIS
>
> He looks like a killer.

> IRIS
>
> I think Cancers make the best lovers. My whole family are air signs.

> TRAVIS
>
> He shoots dope too.

> IRIS
>
> What makes you so high and mighty? Did you ever look at your own eyeballs in a mirror? You don't get eyes like that from . . .

TRAVIS

He's worse than an animal. Jail's too good for scum like
that.

*There is a brief silence. Iris's mind whirls at 78 rpm. She seems to
have three subjects on her mind at a time. She welcomes this opportunity to unburden herself.*

IRIS

Rock music died in 1970, that's what I think. Before that it
was fantastic. I can tell you that. Everybody was crashing,
hanging out at the Fillmore. Me and my girlfriend Ann
used to go up the fire escape, you know? It was unbelievable. Rock stars everywhere. The Airplane – that's my
group, man. All Libras. But now everybody's split or got
sick or busted. I think I'll move to one of those communes
in Vermont, you know? That's where all the smart ones
went. I stayed here.

TRAVIS

I never been to a commune. I don't know. I saw pictures
in a magazine, and it didn't look very clean to me.

IRIS

Why don't you come to a commune with me?

TRAVIS

Me? I could never go to a place like that.

IRIS

Why not?

TRAVIS
(*hesitant*)

I . . . I don't get along with people like that.

IRIS

You a Scorpian? That's it. You're a Scorpian. I can tell.

TRAVIS

Besides, I've got to stay here.

                              IRIS

Why?

                             TRAVIS

I've got something important to do. I can't leave.

                              IRIS

What's so important?

                             TRAVIS

I can't say – it's top secret. I'm doing something for the
Army. The cab thing is just part-time.

                              IRIS

You a narc?

                             TRAVIS

Do I look like a narc?

                              IRIS

Yeah.

Travis breaks out in his big infectious grin, and Iris joins his laughter.

God, I don't know who's weirder, you or me.

                             TRAVIS
                            (*pause*)

What are you going to do about Sport and that old bastard?

                              IRIS

When?

                             TRAVIS

When you leave.

                              IRIS

Just leave 'em. There's plenty of other girls.

                             TRAVIS

You just gonna leave 'em?

IRIS
(*astonished*)
What should I do? Call the cops?

TRAVIS
Cops don't do nothin'.

IRIS
Sport never treated me bad, honest. Never beat me up once.

TRAVIS
You can't leave 'em to do the same to other girls. You should get rid of them.

IRIS
How?

TRAVIS
(*shrugs*)
I don't know. Just should, though.
(*pause*)
Somebody should kill 'em. Nobody'd miss 'em.

IRIS
(*taken aback*)
God. I know where they should have a commune for you. They should have a commune for you at Bellevue.

TRAVIS
(*apologetic/sheepish*)
I'm sorry, Iris. I didn't mean that.

IRIS
You're not much with girls, are you?

TRAVIS
(*thinks*)
Well, Iris, I look at it this way. A lot of girls come into my cab, some of them very beautiful. And I figure all day long men have been after them: trying to touch them, talk to them, ask them out. And they hate it. So I figure the best I

can do for them is not to bother them at all. So I don't say
a thing. I pretend I'm not even there. I figure they'll
understand that and appreciate me for it.

*It takes Iris a moment to digest this pure example of negative think-
ing: I am loved to the extent I do not exist.*

IRIS

Do you really think I should go to the commune?

TRAVIS

I think you should go home, but otherwise I think you
should go. It would be great for you. You have to get away
from here. The city's a sewer, you gotta get out of it.

*Mumbling something about her 'shades' again, Iris fishes through
her bag until she comes up with another 99¢ pair of sunglasses and
puts them on. She likes these better, she decides.*

IRIS

Sure you don't want to come with me?

TRAVIS

I can't. Otherwise, I would.

IRIS

I sure hate to go alone.

TRAVIS

I'll give you the money to go. I don't want you to take any
from those guys.

IRIS

You don't have to.

TRAVIS

I want to – what else can I do with my money?
(*thinks*)
You may not see me again – for a while.

IRIS

What do you mean?

Close-up of Travis.

TRAVIS

My work may take me out of New York.

Iris's room. Day.

Sport stands beside the bed.

SPORT

What's the matter, baby, don't you feel right?

Iris is wearing her blue-tinted shades.

IRIS

It's my stomach. I got the flu.

Sport puts his hands on her hips. He is slowly, carefully, smoothly manipulating her. It's the stoned black hustle.

SPORT

Oh, baby, there ain't no flu. You know that, baby.

IRIS

Honest, Sport.

Sport puts some slow soul music on the stereo.

SPORT

You're just tired, baby. You just need your man. I am your man, you know. You are my woman. I wouldn't be nothing without you.

Sport slowly grinds his hips to hers. Iris starts to move with him. This is what she really wanted. Her man's attention.

I know this may not mean anything to you, baby, but sometimes I get so emotional, sometimes I think, I wish every man could have what I have now, that every woman could be loved the way I love you. I wish every man could be as happy with his woman as I am with you now. I go home and I think what it would be without you, and then I thank God for you. I think to myself, man, you are so lucky. You got a woman who loves you, who needs you, a woman who keeps you strong. It's just you and me. I'm nothing without you. I can go like this for ever and ever. We can do it, baby. You and me. Just you and me.

Sport slowly rubs his crotch into her. Iris smiles. She is happy. The music rises.

GOD'S LONELY MAN

Firing range. Day. Travis stands at the firing range blasting the .44 Magnum with a rapid-fire vengeance.

He puts down one gun, picks up the next, then the next. Quickly reloading, he fires again.

The targets spin and dance under his barrage. The piercing sound of gunshots rings through the air.

Inside Travis's apartment.

Travis is again writing at the table. His western shirt is open, exposing his bare chest.

A note of despair and doom has entered into Travis's normally monotone narration voice: this will be the last entry in his diary.

TRAVIS (V.O.)
My whole life has pointed in one direction. I see that now. There never has been any choice for me.

Lengthy point-of-view shot from Travis's taxi: we see New York's nightlife as Travis sees it. Camera tracks down midtown sidewalks in slightly slow motion. There we see couples, walking in slowing motion: young couples, middle-aged couples, old couples, hookers and johns, girlfriends, boyfriends, business friends – the whole world matched up in pairs, and Travis left wandering alone in the night.

Others would notice the breasts, the asses, the faces, but not Travis: he notices the girl's hand that rubs the hair on her boyfriend's neck, the hand that hangs lightly on his shoulder, the nuzzling kiss in the ear.

Loneliness has followed me all my life. The life of loneliness pursues me wherever I go: in bars, cars, coffee shops, theaters, stores, sidewalks. There is no escape. I am God's lonely man.

Travis's point-of-view: another neighborhood, later in the night. Still in slightly slow motion. The crowds are more sparse here, the streets darker, a junkie shudders in a doorway, a wino pukes into a trash can, a street-walker meets a prospective client.

I am not a fool. I will no longer fool myself. I will no longer let myself fall apart, become a joke and object of ridicule. I know there is no longer any hope. I cannot continue this hollow, empty fight. I must sleep. What hope is there for me?

Inside Travis's apartment.

Travis, his shirt fastened, stands beside table. Close-up: he lays a brief hand-written letter on the table. We read it.

Dear Iris,
This money should be enough for
your trip. By the time you read
this I will be dead.
Travis

Travis stacks five crisp hundred-dollar bills beside the letter, folds them up with the letter, and puts them into an envelope.

A short while later. Travis has cleaned up his apartment. Everything is neat and orderly.

Camera pans across room: the mattress is bare and flattened out, the floor is spotless, the cans and bottles of food and pills put out of sight. The wall is still covered with Palantine political paraphernalia, but when we reach the desk we see only four items there: an open diary and three loaded revolvers: .44, .38, .25.

Travis, freshly shaved and neatly dressed, stands in the middle of his clean room. The empty holster hangs on his shoulder. Metal .25 gliders can be seen under the slit in his right sleeve. He turns toward table.

Travis, envelope in hand, closes the door behind him and walks down the corridor.

He passes an open door and we are surprised to see the room is empty – and trashed. Travis lives in a decaying, if not condemned, building.

Outside, Travis places the envelope to Iris in his mail box.

Back in apartment, camera closes on revolvers lying on the table in neat array.

THERE IS AN ASSASSIN

Sound of a political rally: cheering, laughing, a band playing, talking.

Afternoon. A crowd of about 500 is assembled before a platform outside a Brooklyn union hall. A Dixieland band is playing on the platform.

Close-up of Charles Palantine's feet climbing out of a limousine. There is a roar from the crowd near by.

Palantine, a bulky secret service man to the right and left of him, pushes his way through the crowd toward the platform. Still cameras click, and TV cameras purr.

Slight timecut: Palantine is speaking on the platform.

Travis's empty taxi sits parked a few blocks away from rally. At this distance, the rally sounds are almost indistinguishable.

Close-up of Travis's boots walking. They make their way past one person, then two, then a cluster of three or four. Sounds of rally increase.

We see a full-figure shot of Travis: he is standing alone in an opening near the fringes of the crowd.

Travis looks like the most suspicious human being alive. His hair is cropped short, he wears mirror-reflecting glasses. His face is pallid and drained of color, his lips are pursed and drawn tight. He looks from side to side. One can now see the full effect of Travis's lack of sleep and insufficient diet – he looks sick and frail.

Even though it is a warm June day, Travis is bundled up in a shirt,

*sweater, and Army jacket buttoned from top to bottom. Under his
jacket are several large lumps, causing his upper torso to look larger
than it should. He is slightly hunched over and his hands shoved
into his pockets.*

*Anyone scanning the crowd would immediately light upon Travis
and think, 'There is an assassin.'*

Travis pulls the vial of red pills from his pocket and swallows a couple.

*The secret service man is standing beside the platform, scanning the
crowd. It is the same secret service man Travis spoke to at the first
rally. Tom, dressed in a conservative suit, stands beside him.
Palantine is wrapping up his short speech.*

PALANTINE
. . . and with your help we will go on to victory at the polls
Tuesday –

Applause.

Travis begins moving up into the crowd.

– on to victory in Miami Beach next month –

Applause mounts.

– and on to victory next November!

*Palantine steps back, smiling and receiving the applause. Then, nod-
ding at the secret service man, he descends the stairs and prepares to
work his way through the crowd. Travis unbuttons the middle two
buttons of his jacket, opening access to his holster. With the other
hand he checks the .44 hooked behind his back.*

*Palantine smiles and shakes a few of the many hands outstretched
toward him.*

*The secret service man, scanning the crowd, spots something that
interests him. He looks closely.*

*Secret service man's point of view: Travis, his face intense, pushes his
way through the crowd. Palantine works his way through the crowd
and cameras.*

Secret service man motions to second secret service man and points in Travis's direction.

Travis slips his hand into his jacket.

The second secret service man converges on Travis from the side.

Travis and Palantine draw closer to each other.

Secret service man, walking just behind Palantine, grabs the candidate's hand and pulls him backwards.

Palantine looks sharply back at the secret service man, who motions for him to take a slightly altered route.

Travis sees this: his eyes meet the secret service man's. He recognizes the situation. To his right he spots the second secret service man.

Travis's eyes meet Palantine's: candidate and would-be assassin exchange quick glances.

Travis hastily works his way back through the crowd. He hears the secret service man's voice call out.

SECRET SERVICE MAN
Detain that man!

Overhead shot reveals Travis has the jump on his pursuers. He is breaking free of the crowd while they are still mired in it. Travis, free of his pursuers, quickly makes his way down the sidewalks. The secret service men look futilely about.

Travis jumps in his cab. Sweat covers his face.

TOWARD THE KILL

The film is moving fast now; it pushes hard and straight toward its conclusion. We're moving toward the kill.

Late afternoon. Travis's taxi skids around a corner and speeds into Manhattan.

Travis checks his mail slot: the letter to Iris has already been picked up by the mailman.

Stripped to the waist, Travis walks back and forth across his apartment wiping his torso with a bath towel.

He begins dressing: he straps the Army combat knife to his calf; he reflexes the metal gliders and the Colt .25 on his right forearm.

Sport stands in his doorway on the Lower East Side. It is early evening. A pudgy middle-aged white private cop walks up to Sport. The two men laugh, slap each other on the back, and exchange a soul shake. They discuss a little private business and the private cop walks off in the direction of Iris's apartment.

Travis straps on holster and fits the .38 Special into it.

Private cop walks down block.

Travis hooks the huge Magnum into the back of his belt. He puts on his Army jacket and walks out through the door.

Private cop turns up darkened stairway to Iris's apartment.

Night has fallen. Travis's taxi careens down 10th Avenue. He speeds, honks, accelerates quickly. The glare of speeding yellow and red lights flash through the night.

Travis's point of view: a pedestrian attempts to flag down the taxi, but quickly steps back up on the curb when he sees Travis has no intention of stopping for anything.

Sport maintains his post in the dark doorway. He waves to a girl who passes, and she waves back.

Travis's taxi screeches to a stop and parks obliquely against the curb.

THE SLAUGHTER

Travis walks down the block to the doorway where Sport stands.

Camera tracks with Travis.

Without slowing down, Travis walks up to Sport and puts his arm on his shoulder in a gesture of friendliness.

TRAVIS

Hey, Sport. How are things?

                              SPORT
                             (*shrugs*)
          OK, cowboy.

                             TRAVIS
                          (*needling him*)
          How are things in the *pimp* business, hey, Sport?

                              SPORT
          What's going on?

                             TRAVIS
          I'm here to see Iris.

                              SPORT
          Iris?

Travis pushes Sport back into the dark recesses of the corridor.

          Wha–?

                             TRAVIS
          Yeah, Iris. You know anybody by that name?

                              SPORT
          No.
                            (*a pause*)
          Hillbilly, you'd better get your wise ass outta here and
          quick, or you're gonna be in trouble.

*Travis is being propelled by an inner force, a force which takes him
past the boundaries of reason and self-control.*

                             TRAVIS
                       (*with restrained anger*)
          You carry a gun?

*Sport looks into Travis's eyes, saying nothing: he realizes the serious-
ness of the situation.*

*Travis pulls his .38 Special and holds it on Sport, pushing him even
further back against the wall.*

          Get it.

SPORT
(*submissive*)

Hey, mister, I don't know what's going on here. This don't make any sense.

TRAVIS
(*demanding*)

Show it to me.

Sport reluctantly pulls a .32 caliber pistol (a 'purse gun') from his pocket and holds it limply.

Travis sticks his .38 into Sport's gut and discharges it. There is a muffled blast, followed by a muted scream of pain.

Now suck on that.

Agony and shock cross Sport's face as he slumps to the floor. Travis turns and walks away before Sport even hits.

As Travis walks away, Sport can be seen struggling in the background.

Travis, his gun slipped into his jacket, walks quickly up the sidewalk.

Around the corner, he walks into the darkened stairway leading to Iris's apartment.

As he walks up the stairs, he pulls the .44 Magnum from behind his back and transfers the .38 Special to his left hand. He walks up the steps, a pistol dangling from each hand. At the top of the stairs, Travis spots the old man sitting at the far end of the dark corridor. The old man starts to get up when Travis discharges the mighty .44 at him. BLAAM! The hallway reverberates with shockwaves and gun powder.

The old man staggers at the end of the corridor: his right hand has been blown off at the forearm.

There is the sharp sound of a gunshot behind Travis: his face grimaces in pain. A bullet has ripped through the left side of his neck. Blood flows over his left shoulder.

Travis's .44 flies into the air.

Travis looks down the stairway: there Sport lies choking in a puddle of his own blood. He has struggled far enough to fire one shot.

Falling, Travis drills another .38 slug into Sport's back, but Sport is already dead.

Travis slumps to his knees. Down the corridor the old man with a bloody stump is struggling toward him. Travis turns his .38 toward the old man.

The door to No. 2 opens: Iris's scream is heard in the background. The bulky frame of the private cop fills the doorway. His blue shirt is open and in his hand hangs a .38 service revolver. The private cop raises his gun and shoots Travis. Travis, blood gushing from his right shoulder, sinks to the floor. His .38 clangs down the stairs.

The old man grows closer. Travis smashes his right arm against the wall; miraculously, the small Colt .25 glides down his forearm into his palm.

Travis fills the private cop's face full of bullet holes.

The private cop, screaming, crashes back into the room.

The old man crashes atop Travis. The .25 falls from Travis's hand.

Both men are bleeding profusely as they thrash into Iris's room. Iris hides behind the old red velvet sofa, her face frozen in fright.

Travis, trapped under the heavy old man, reaches down with his right hand and pulls the combat knife from his right calf. Just as Travis draws back the knife, the old man brings his huge left palm crashing down on Travis: the old man's palm is impaled on the knife.

The old man screams in pain.

Police sirens are heard in the background.

With a great effort, Travis turns over, pinning the old man to the floor. The bloody knife blade sticks through his upturned hand.

Travis reaches over with his right hand and picks up the revolver of the now dead private cop.

He hoists himself up and sticks the revolver into the old man's mouth.

The old man's voice is full of pain and ghastly fright:

OLD MAN
Don't kill me! Don't kill me!

Iris screams in background. Travis looks up.

IRIS
Don't kill him, Travis! Don't kill him!

Travis fires the revolver, blowing the back of the old man's head off and silencing his protests.

The police sirens screech to a halt. Sound of police officers running up the stairs.

Travis struggles up and collapses on the red velvet sofa, his blood-soaked body blending with the velvet.

Iris retreats in fright against the far wall.

First uniformed police officer rushes into room, drawn gun in hand. Other policemen can be heard running up the stairs.

Travis looks helplessly up at the officer. He forms his bloody hand into a pistol, raises it to his forehead and, his voice croaking in pain, makes the sound of a pistol discharging.

TRAVIS
Pgghew! Pgghew!

Out-of-breath fellow officers join the first policeman. They survey the room.

Travis's head slumps against the sofa.

Iris is huddled in the corner, shaking.

Live sound ceases. Overhead slow-motion tracking shot surveys the damage: from Iris shaking against the blood-spattered wall; to Travis's blood-soaked body lying on the sofa; to the old man with half a head, a bloody stump for one hand, and a knife sticking out of the other; to police officers staring in amazement; to the private cop's bullet-ridden face trapped near the doorway; to puddles of blood and a lonely .44 Magnum lying on the hallway carpet; down

the blood-speckled stairs on which lies a nickel-plated .38 Smith and
Wesson Special; to the foot of the stairs where Sport's body is
hunched over a pool of blood and a small .32 lies near his hand; to
crowds huddled around the doorway, held back by police officers;
past red flashing lights, running policemen and parked police cars; to
the ongoing nightlife of the Lower East Side, curious but basically
unconcerned, looking then heading its own way. *

LETTER FROM PITTSBURGH

Outside Travis's apartment. Day. It is early autumn. The trees are
losing their leaves.

Slow tracking shot across inside of apartment. Room appears pretty
much the same, although there is a new portable TV and an inex-
pensive easy chair.

[Visual]	[Audio]
Track begins at table and works across room to the mattress. We see these items: On the table rests the diary, closed. A desk calendar stands on the table: it is October. Across the wall, where the Palantine clippings once hung, there are now a series of new newspaper clippings. They read from right to left. The first is a full back page from the New York Daily News. *Headline reads:* 'CABBIE BATTLES GANGSTERS.' *There are large photos of police stand-*	Throughout the track, we hear the voice of a middle-aged un-educated man reading in voice-over. It is the voice of Iris's father, reading a letter he sent to Travis, and which Travis has tacked to his wall.
	IRIS'S FATHER (V.O.) 'Dear Mr Bickle, I can't say how happy Mrs Steensma and I were to hear that you are well and recuperating. We tried to visit you at

*Screenwriter's note: The screenplay has been moving at a reasonably realistic level until this prolonged slaughter. The slaughter itself is a gory extension of violence, more surreal than real.

  The slaughter is the moment Travis has been heading for all his life, and where this screenplay has been heading for over 115 pages. It is the release of all that cumulative pressure; it is a reality unto itself. It is the psychopath's Second Coming.

ing in Iris's room after the slaughter, and a picture of Travis's cabbie mug shot. Underneath this there is a more discreet clipping, without a photo, from the New York Times. *Two-column headline reads:* 'CABBIE SHOOT-OUT, THREE DEAD.'
A follow-up story from the News: *two-column photo shows a plain middle-aged couple sitting in a middle-class living room. Two-column headline reads:* 'PARENTS EXPRESS SHOCK, GRATITUDE.'
A two-column Daily News *story without photo. Headline reads:* 'TAXI-DRIVER HERO TO RECOVER.'
A one-column two-paragraph News *story stuck on an obscure page. Headline reads:* 'CABBIE RETURNS TO JOB.'
At the end of the clippings, a letter is tacked to the wall. It is a simple letter, handwritten on plain white paper. The handwriting belongs to someone who has made a conscious effort to appear neat and orderly. We recognize from some of the words that it is the same letter that is being read in voice over. When we finally arrive at the mattress, we find it is barren. A pillow and blanket (new purchases) are folded at the head of the bed.

the hospital when we were in New York to pick up Iris, but you were still in a coma.

There is no way we can repay you for returning our Iris to us. We thought we had lost her, but now our lives are full again. Needless to say, you are something of a hero around this household.

I'm sure you want to know about Iris. She is back in school and working hard. The transition has been very hard for her, as you can well imagine, but we have taken steps to see she never has cause to run away again.

In conclusion, Mrs Steensma and I would like to again thank you from the bottom of our hearts. Unfortunately, we cannot afford to come to New York again to thank you in person, or we surely would. But if you should ever come to Pittsburgh, you would find yourself a most welcome guest in our home.

Our deepest thanks,
Burt and Ivy Steensma'

OLD FRIENDS

Outside the Plaza Hotel. Night.

Four cabs stand in the waiting line in front of the hotel.

Near the entrance, Travis and Wizard stand in the light, talking.

Travis's hair is almost fully grown back to its normal length. He wears the same clothes – cowboy boots, jeans, western shirt, Army jacket – but he isn't wearing a gun. There is a thick scar on the left side of his neck.

Wizard is speaking.

> WIZARD
>
> A private owner wanted to swap wheels. Now my tires were brand new. 'Give me a couple days,' I says.

Charlie T parks his cab in line and walks toward Travis and Wizard.

> CHARLIE T
>
> Howdy, Wizard, Killer.

Charlie T points his pistol/finger at Travis, fires, says 'Pow,' and laughs.

> (*casual joking*)
>
> Don't mess with the Killer.

> TRAVIS
> (*smiles*)
>
> Hey, Charlie T.

> WIZARD
>
> Howsit, Charlie?
> (*a pause*)
> Hey, Travis, I think you gotta fare.

They all turn. Point-of-view shot of doorman closing rear door of Travis's taxi.

> TRAVIS
>
> Shit.

He runs off.

CHARLIE T

Take it slow, Killer.

Travis waves back to Charlie T and Wizard as he runs around cab and jumps in the driver's seat.

His taxi pulls away.

Close-up of Travis at the wheel. From the back, a female voice says:

FEMALE VOICE

34 East 56th Street.

Travis recognizes the voice. He looks in the rear-view mirror: it is Betsy.

Travis says nothing: he heads toward 56th Street. After a silence, Betsy speaks.

BETSY

Hello, Travis.

TRAVIS

Hello, Betsy.

There is an uneasy pause.

I see where Palantine got the nomination.

BETSY

Yes. It won't be long now. Seventeen days.

TRAVIS

Well, I hope he wins.

There is another pause.

BETSY
(*concerned*)

How are *you*, Travis? I read about you in the papers.

TRAVIS

Oh, I got over that. It was nothing, really. The papers always blow these things up.

(*a pause*)
A little stiffness. That'll go away. I just sleep more, that's all.

Travis's taxi pulls up at 34 East 56th Street.

Here we are.

Betsy digs in her purse.

(*protesting*)
No, no, please. This fare's on me. Please.

BETSY
Thank you, Travis.

Betsy gets out of the cab and stands by the right front window, which is open.

Travis prepares to drive away.

Travis?

TRAVIS
Yeah?

BETSY
Maybe I'll see you again sometime, huh?

TRAVIS
(*with a thin smile*)
Sure.

Betsy steps away from the curb and Travis drives off. She watches his taxi.

Camera follows Travis's taxi as it slowly disappears down 56th Street.

American Gigolo

CAST AND CREW

MAIN CAST

JULIAN KAY	Richard Gere
MICHELLE STRATTON	Lauren Hutton
DETECTIVE SUNDAY	Hector Elizondo
ANNE	Nina Van Pallandt
LEON JAIMES	Bill Duke
CHARLES STRATTON	Brian Davies
LISA WILLIAMS	K. Callan
MR RHYMAN	Tom Stewart
JUDY RHYMAN	Patti Carr
LIEUTENANT CURTIS	David Cryer

MAIN CREW

Directed by	Paul Schrader
Screenplay by	Paul Schrader
Produced by	Jerry Bruckheimer
Executive Producer	Freddie Fields
Cinematography by	John Bailey
Film Editing by	Richard Halsey
Production Design by	Ferdinando Scarfiotti
Richard Gere's costumes by	Giorgio Armani
Music by	Giorgio Moroder

'The idea of a duty to be performed, and the fear of making himself ridiculous if he failed to perform it, immediately removed all pleasure from his heart.'

— of Julien Sorel in
The Red and the Black

Julian Kay, twenty-six, boyish, sensual, professional. His features are lean, hard. Razor-like.

At first his movements seem disjointed: the legs too loose, the hips too high, the chin slightly turned. Then you see the pattern. Every gesture is calculated to attract attention.

Scratching his ear, massaging his wrists, smoothing the flat of his palm across his buttocks.

His eyes flit out at you, you turn your head, he smiles. You try to turn away, but cannot. He smiles again.

Julian is on the prowl. He is looking: for a trick, a companion, someone to please.

Yet all the while he is heading toward love.

FADE IN:

Pre-credits.

INT. COCKTAIL LOUNGE — NIGHT

We only see his face, speaking through the shadows.

He brushes his index finger lightly across his lips as he speaks. He knows: *his lips are his most sexual organ.*

> JULIAN
>
> You know who I am. I know who you are. We have no secrets. I know what you're thinking. You know what I'm thinking. We have our own methods of communication. You don't have to say anything. I can read your thoughts. I know what you need. You're afraid. You're afraid of your husband. You're afraid of yourself. You're afraid of your own sexuality. You're afraid to ask for what you need. You're afraid of being hurt.

Julian sits in a dimly lit booth with a middle-aged woman. His eyes are only on her. His crème brûlée is untouched.

The woman nervously sips her coffee as he spins his web.

> There's no reason to be afraid. I don't know why you're afraid. I don't even know why we're sitting here. Why we're wasting time eating things we don't want to eat, doing things we don't want to do, talking in front of people who don't matter. It's so simple. You know who I am. You want to be here. You want to be with me. You know what I can do. I can make you relax, relax like you've never relaxed before. Make you aroused like you've never been aroused before. Excited. I know how to touch you. Where to touch you. How to kiss you. Where to kiss you . . .

> CUT TO:

End pre-credits.

Credits.

EXT. BEVERLY HILLS — DAY

Julian pulls his black Mercedes 450SL to the curb, gets out, and opens the door for the middle-aged woman.

They walk into Juschi's.

> CUT TO:

INT. JUSCHI'S — DAY

A gracious salesman slips Julian into a cashmere sports jacket. He has already set aside two dark three-piece suits.

Julian examines the fit of his tan gabardine slacks in the three-way mirror.

He watches as the woman signs a charge slip. The salesman sets Julian's clothes aside.

> CUT TO:

EXT. COAST HIGHWAY — DAY

Julian's black convertible snakes up the Malibu coast. The morning sun glistens across the Pacific.

    CUT TO:

EXT. MALIBU HOME — DAY

The middle-aged woman kisses Julian and closes the door behind him.

He gets into his car and drives off.

    CUT TO:

EXT. COAST HIGHWAY — DAY

Julian slips a cassette of Johnny Hallyday's Super Hits *into the stereo and turns up the volume:* 'Celui quit'a fait pleurer.'

    CUT TO:

EXT. ANNE'S HOUSE — DAY

Julian pulls into another Malibu driveway, gets out, and enters a beach house.

    CUT TO:

End credits.

INT. ANNE'S HOUSE — DAY

Julian walks through the comfortable beach house. Expensive antiques and prints offset white rattan beach furniture.

Two topless women are sunning themselves on the deck. Julian walks out and joins them.

               JULIAN

  Hello, girls.

Anne, an attractive woman in her mid-thirties, welcomes him enthusiastically.

ANNE

Julian! You came all the way out here. It's been weeks.

JULIAN
(*shrugs and smiles*)

I had to drop somebody off up the beach so I thought I'd drop by. Hello, girls.

Anne's companions, Beth and Judy, both about twenty, girls of extraordinary and vacuous beauty, greet him more coolly.

BETH
(*sarcastic*)

You mean you didn't fly down to Rio for the weekend?

Anne dismisses them with a wave of her hand.

ANNE

Don't mind those cunts. They're just jealous.

Anne leads Julian into the house. She doesn't bother to put a top on.

I've been trying to reach you all day.

JULIAN

I got the message. A trick?

He helps himself to a can of diet soda.

ANNE

Tonight. A woman from Charlottesville. She's flying in to close a negotiation on her husband's estate.

JULIAN
(*drinking soda*)

First time?

ANNE

Yeah. She's meeting with Smith, Silberman, and Hancock in the morning. They want a chauffeur.

JULIAN

That's cool. A thousand?

Anne nods.

> 600 for me.

> ANNE
> Awh, Julie, don't start this up again.

> JULIAN
> You like fifty–fifty? Why don't you get Mike or one of those high-school dropouts you like so much.

> ANNE
> There's no percentage in it if I don't get fifty–fifty. You already cut me out of the repeaters.

> JULIAN
> That's only fair.

> ANNE
> It ain't fair, but I ain't got any choice.

> JULIAN
> Of course you do. You can keep dealing those uneducated fags . . .

> ANNE
> (*interrupting*)
> Look who's talking.

> JULIAN
> (*ignoring her*)
> . . . who don't know class from ass. All right, fifty–fifty.

> ANNE
> Who did you drop off up the beach?

> JULIAN
> (*teasing*)
> Wouldn't you like to know?

> ANNE
> Aw, Julie, why do you do this to me?

JULIAN

You know somebody else that can get into the LA Country Club? – and that's not the Hillcrest. I gotta run now.
Leave the info on my service.

He turns to leave.

ANNE

You don't want to take some sun?

JULIAN
(*gestures*)
Not with those bitches. They'll eat a man up.

Beth cocks her head and calls back.

BETH

That's more than you'd ever do.

JULIAN
(*to Anne*)
No class. Catch you later, Anne.

Anne calls to him as he leaves.

ANNE

How's the Swedish coming?

CUT TO:

EXT. LIMO – EVENING

*Julian straightens his jacket and slides the glass partition open. Mrs
Dobrun, a well-dressed woman about fifty, looks with wonderment
at the LA night landscape.*

Julian turns and looks at Mrs Dobrun.

JULIAN

May I take off my cap, ma'am?

MRS DOBRUN
(*smiles*)

Of course.

JULIAN

Thank you.

He places his cap on the seat. He runs his hand through his hair as he glances at Mrs Dobrun in the mirror. She is watching him.

The black limousine speeds up the San Diego freeway.

CUT TO:

EXT. BEVERLY HILLS HOTEL — EVENING

Julian pulls the limo into the hotel drive.

While the doorman opens the door for Mrs Dobrun, Julian runs around the car and takes out her luggage.

Before the porter can protest, Julian slips a folded bill into his palm. Julian carries Mrs Dobrun's luggage into the hotel.

CUT TO:

INT. MRS DOBRUN'S SUITE — EVENING

A bucket of iced champagne and a basket of fruit wait on the table. Julian's manner is overly polite, almost apologetic.

JULIAN

I think I know this hotel even better than my own apartment. It's where the important people stay. I used to be a pool boy here.

Mrs Dobrun opens a suitcase.

You want me to help you with anything? Here, I'll open the champagne.

MRS DOBRUN

Look, ah, you don't . . .

JULIAN
(*opening champagne*)

My name's Julian.

MRS DOBRUN

You don't have to open the champagne. I'll give you a tip.
Don't worry.

JULIAN
(*abject*)

Oh, Jesus, I'm sorry, Mrs Dobrun. That's not what I
meant at all. I'm just trying to do my job right. Sometimes
people complain.

MRS DOBRUN

I'm sorry.

JULIAN

Is this your first trip to LA?

MRS DOBRUN

Maybe you *can* help me.

JULIAN

Yes?

MRS DOBRUN

I haven't been here in several years . . . and I was wonder-
ing if there were any new really good restaurants, you
know, where the, ah, famous people go.

JULIAN

It's safer to recommend the established restaurants: Ma
Maison, Scandia, La Scala. But of the newer ones, I hear
Le Dome is quite popular.

He still holds the open champagne bottle.

MRS DOBRUN

You're making me thirsty just standing there. Pour me a
drink and set the bottle down.

Julian pours her a glass.

*The more we see of Julian Kay, the less we understand him. He can
be many things to many people. He seeks out the pleasure they
desire, then provides it. He can be sweet, consoling, cool, intellectual,*

kind, earnest, arrogant – and all the while remain something beyond all his poses: a mysterious sexual force.

CUT TO:

INT. HOTEL LOBBY – NIGHT

Julian is on the phone in the hotel lobby.

>   JULIAN
>   (*on phone*)
> Fuck, I don't know anything about that. But – I'm not
> sure – I don't think Mrs Dobrun's hold on the tobacco
> people is that strong. In fact, I'm sure of it. She seemed
> worried about that. She may settle short.
>   (*beat*)
> I don't know. She's a nice woman. Look, I'm supposed to
> meet her here tomorrow at 12.30. Whatever she's doing in
> the morning, she's gonna be finished by noon.
>   (*beat*)
> OK, Anne, love you too.
>   (*beat*)
> Don't worry. I'll be ready.

He steps out of the phone booth, removes his coat and cap and exchanges them for his regular sports jacket at the cloak room. He tips the girl and flirts with her. She knows him.

CUT TO:

INT. COCKTAIL LOUNGE – NIGHT

Straightening his jacket, Julian steps into the cocktail lounge. He slips a bill into the maître d's *palm and chats with him a moment before finding a seat.*

Julian orders a drink and checks out the lounge. He studies the room for potential customers: the pickings are slim. He sips his Manhattan.

Then he sees her: even with her back half-turned, her beauty is apparent. Blonde hair, about thirty. She has been waiting. Drinking

*and waiting. For what? Something to change her life? Something.
Julian senses this.*

*She speaks to the waiter in a foreign language. He listens closely. It
seems to be French.*

*Julian gets up and, drink in hand, walks over to her table. She turns
as he approaches.*

JULIAN
*Excusez-moi, puis-je m'assoir un instant. J'ai surpris votre
conversation . . .*

MICHELLE
Mais bien sur.

JULIAN
(introducing himself)
Je m'appelle Julian Kay.

MICHELLE
Excusez-moi. Michelle Jost.

JULIAN
Enchanté.

MICHELLE
(notices his glass)
Est-ce-que je peux vous offrir quelque chose?

Julian sits.

JULIAN
Avec plaisir.

Michelle waves the waiter over.

MICHELLE
Mr Kay would like another drink. *Qu'est-ce que vous
prenez?*

Michelle's fluent English takes Julian aback.

JULIAN
Manhattan. Dry Manhattan on the rocks.

The waiter takes the order and leaves.

You speak English?

MICHELLE

You speak English?

JULIAN

You had me fooled.

MICHELLE

And you me.

JULIAN

How long have you been in Los Angeles?

MICHELLE

I live here.

JULIAN

You live here? I don't understand.

MICHELLE

You wouldn't. I am trying to refresh my college French. I usually practice with a friend, but she hasn't arrived yet.
                    (*beat*)
Where are you from?

JULIAN

I was born in Torino. But I studied at NATS.

MICHELLE

You don't have any accent at all.

JULIAN

I've been traveling too much.

MICHELLE

I envy you. I used to travel a lot, but now my husband is involved in local politics. He thinks it's chic to have a bilingual wife. So I practice French.

Julian is doubly taken aback. First, he thought Michelle could not speak English. Second, he thought she was unattached.

He gulps down his drink and places a five-dollar bill on the table.

JULIAN

I think he's right.

MICHELLE

Where are you going?

JULIAN

I made a mistake.

MICHELLE

My husband's in New York.

JULIAN

No, I made an even bigger mistake than that.

Michelle is confused. She assumed Julian would be more persistent.

MICHELLE

Huh?

JULIAN

You wouldn't understand.

MICHELLE

Why?

JULIAN

I've got to go.

MICHELLE

Where?

JULIAN
(*shrugs*)

I don't know. Home. Pips.

MICHELLE

I've got no place special to go.

JULIAN

What about your friend?

MICHELLE

I'm not waiting for anyone.

JULIAN

You still don't understand.

MICHELLE

Understand what?

Julian feels awkward, embarrassed. He has made a mistake; but why doesn't he just get up and leave? Something about Michelle holds him.

JULIAN

Understand who I am.

MICHELLE

Who are you?

JULIAN

You don't even understand who you are. Why you're here. Why you're sitting in that chair.

MICHELLE

Why are *you* here?

Julian starts to rise.

JULIAN

I've got to go.

Michelle holds his hand.

MICHELLE

Wait. Just tell me one thing: why did you come on to me?

JULIAN

Like I said, I made a mistake. I heard you speaking in French. Often in big hotels you meet women from foreign countries who need a translator or guide and will hire you.

MICHELLE

How many languages do you speak?

JULIAN

Five or six.

MICHELLE
Plus the international language.

JULIAN
That's right.

MICHELLE
(*catching on, sarcastic*)
You're really something special, aren't you?

Julian answers her in kind.

JULIAN
You're one to talk. I saw you sitting here. You *wanted* me
to come over. I know what I see.

MICHELLE
How much would you have charged me?

JULIAN
As a translator or a guide?

MICHELLE
No. Just a straight fuck.

JULIAN
Now you've made a mistake. I don't do that.

MICHELLE
Oh, no? I know what I see, too.

Ever polite, Julian stands.

JULIAN
It's been a pleasure talking to you, Madame Jost. Don't
spoil it. *Bonne chance.*

He turns and walks off. He nods to the maître d' *as he exits.*

*Michelle watches him as he goes. She is befuddled, hurt. Yet also
intrigued, excited.*

CUT TO:

EXT. WESTWOOD APARTMENT HOTEL — DAY

A car waits in front of the Westwood Apartment Hotel. Julian enters.

CUT TO:

INT. JULIAN'S APARTMENT — DAY

Julian's room, like his mind, is eclectic.

Stacks of half-read books and magazines are scattered across his large unmade bed. Cassettes and records are mixed with shoes and shirts. A cold cup of coffee sits on the Times *crossword.*

A Ruscha print hangs on one wall. On another is a chart illustrating styles of nineteenth-century furniture.

Every object is an extension of his probing mind: always curious, always learning, always assimilating. Always improving his craft.

Julian, wearing jeans and a T-shirt, lies on his Universal bench press.

A Berlitz 'Learn Swedish' tape is on his stereo. Julian repeats after the cassette.

> CASSETTE
> I am not interested in that.
> > *(beat)*
> *Jag ar inte intresserad av det.*

> JULIAN
> > *(lifting barbells)*
> I am not interested in that.
> > *(beat)*
> *Jag ar inte intresserad av det.*

> CASSETTE
> How much farther have we to go?
> > *(beat)*
> *Hur manga rum, trapsteg ar det?*

> JULIAN
> How much farther have we to go?
> > *(beat)*

Hur manga rum, trapsteg ar det?

The phone rings. Julian waits. It rings again. He crawls on to the bed and picks up the receiver.

Yeah, put him through.
                    (*beat*)
Hey, Leon. What's up?

A black man's voice comes across the phone.

                    LEON (V.O.)
Julian, baby, I hate to bug you like this, but you gotta help me out. I had this Palm Springs gig set up for tonight for Joey, and the guy takes a powder, or at least he ain't nowhere around.

                    JULIAN
I can't do it. I get a haircut now . . .
                    (*looks at fingernails*)
. . . and I got a thing this afternoon.

                    LEON (V.O.)
Baby, baby, it's a two-hour gig . . .

                    JULIAN
Plus the drive.

                    LEON (V.O.)
Plus the drive. Five Cs. Straight in-and-out job. Do a brother a favor.

                    JULIAN
Well, maybe – if I get free. I'll give you fifty bucks.

                    LEON (V.O.)
Fuck that, Jack. You think I'm in the charity business?

                    JULIAN
Hey, hey, who's doin' who the favor here? Who just called up who beggin' for a sub?

                    LEON (V.O.)
OK, baby, I'm sorry. I appreciate it.

> JULIAN

Anything for a friend. Call back and give the service the info. I'm bad with details.

> LEON (V.O.)

Thanks, bro.

Julian gets another line and flashes the desk:

> JULIAN

Jill, get me an appointment at Sassoon's in forty-five minutes and tell the maid she can make the room up in an hour.

CUT TO:

EXT. INTERSTATE 10 — EVENING

Julian's black Mercedes heads west.

CUT TO:

EXT. PALM SPRINGS — EVENING

Julian pulls into the drive of an expensive Palm Springs home.

INT. PALM SPRINGS HOME — NIGHT

Julian, straightening his tan polished cotton suit, argues with Mr Rhyman, a fortyish businessman, in the living room of Rhyman's nouveau riche home. Rhyman wears gabardine slacks and Gucci loafers.

> JULIAN
> (*holding up hands*)

Hey, baby, somebody's made a mistake. I don't do fags. I don't do couples.

Rhyman is nervous. He has had several drinks.

> RHYMAN

No, no, you don't understand. It's just my wife. Judy. Not me. Just her.

> JULIAN
> (*nods*)

OK.

> RHYMAN

But can I watch?

> JULIAN

Of course.

Rhyman motions toward the bar.

> RHYMAN

Would you like a drink?

> JULIAN

No.

Julian starts to unbutton his shirt. Rhyman stops him.

> RHYMAN

Not yet.

Julian slowly slips one button back into its hole, teasing Rhyman with his eyes.

> JULIAN

You'll have to pay me now.

> RHYMAN
> (*digging into pocket*)

Sure, sure.

He slips Julian the folded bills.

I like to talk afterwards too.

Julian nods and heads toward the bedroom.

CUT TO:

INT. RHYMAN BEDROOM — NIGHT

Julian takes his jacket off and drapes it over the back of a chair. He looks across the brightly lit room.

Judy, Rhyman's wife, lies naked under a sheet. It's not clear whether she's afraid or aroused – or both.

Julian unbuttons his shirt as he sits next to Judy. A gold statuette stands on the night stand.

Rhyman stands against the wall across the room.

Julian speaks softly to Judy, as if they are the only ones in the room. In his mind they are: he is not interested in Rhyman.

> JULIAN
> (*sing-song*)
> Hello, Judy. You're a very sexy lady. You're a very good-looking woman. You're going to like me. We're going to have a lot of fun.
> (*slips off shoes*)
> I can tell. I like you. Just lie back and relax. Close your eyes. Let your mind run free. You'll like this.

He drops his trousers to the floor. Judy seems afraid.

> Don't worry, baby. I know what you want. I know how to take care of you.
> (*touching her*)
> You have a very firm, beautiful body. Close your eyes, baby.

Julian pulls the sheet down her naked body. He shelters her eyes from the light and whispers in her ear:

> Just ignore him. This has nothing to do with him. It's just you and me.

Rhyman calls from across the room.

> RHYMAN
> No, no. From behind. It has to be from behind.

Julian looks at Judy; she shows no reaction. He slips one hand under her body.

> JULIAN
> C'mon, baby, just flip on your stomach.

Julian turns her over. He kisses her cheek softly.

> (*whispers*)
> Don't worry. Leave everything to me. I'll get you wet. I
> can take care of you. I know how to do this . . .

> RHYMAN
> (*calling out*)
> Now slap her! Slap that cunt!

*Judy braces for the blow. Julian studies her face a moment. She has
been here before.*

*Julian looks at Rhyman in a cold, degrading manner; then turns at
Judy and looks at her in an equally cold manner. He raises his hand.*

> Now hit her!

He slaps her. Rhyman winces.

> CUT TO:

EXT. BEVERLY HILLS — DAY

Julian, wearing a summer outfit, walks into Juschi's.

> CUT TO:

INT. JUSCHI'S — DAY

*Julian smiles and puts his hand on the salesman's shoulder as they
walk toward the cash register.*

> JULIAN
> I decided to keep the sweater.

> SALESMAN
> I didn't think you would keep all that stuff. It wasn't your
> style.

*The salesman puts a beige cashmere sweater into a bag and hands it
to Julian. He counts a stack of bills and puts them into an envelope:*

> Eight hundred, eight-twenty, eight-thirty. Seventy per cent
> on eleven hundred and eighty.

> JULIAN

Fair enough. Thanks, Mario.

Julian slips the envelope into his vest pocket and starts for the door.

CUT TO:

EXT. DAISY — DAY

Julian walks up Rodeo to the Daisy and steps into the outdoor café.

He spots Leon, a stocky black pimp, and sits down with him. He places his books on the table top.

Leon has little of the gaudy flash associated with the term 'pimp.' A casual passerby would instead take him for an ex-football player turned actor. He has traded in his Mack coat and hat for the Beverly Hills casual/chic look. But traces of the pimp remain – gold necklace and bracelets, a pair of red snakeskin boots.

Next to Julian, he is a shadow of style.

> JULIAN

Hey, Leon.

> LEON

Julie.

Julian removes his jacket and situates his chair to take maximum advantage of the sun.

He pulls out several folded bills, counts off fifty, and gives them to Leon.

> Thanks for helping me out. I finally found Joey holed up with one of his boyfriends.

> JULIAN

Don't mention it.

A pretty waitress smiles at Julian.

> WAITRESS

Hello, Julian.

                              JULIAN
Hi. Just Perrier, thank you.

She walks off.

                              LEON
You made quite a hit in Palm Springs. They want you to
come back.

*Julian, rubbing his eye, looks away. Two girls, dressed by Anne
Klein, laugh at a nearby table.*

I'm serious. They want you back this week. I told 'em I'd
try.

*Julian just shrugs. The waitress brings his Perrier water and walks
off.*

I wouldn't take much 'cause these are regulars for me.

                              JULIAN
I don't know. Maybe.

                              LEON
Principles?

                              JULIAN
It's a long drive, Leon. Besides, I don't like to play the
same numbers too often. People think they own you.
Nobody owns me.

                              LEON
That include Anne?

                              JULIAN
Anne who?

                              LEON
I don't know why you fool with that bitch.

                              JULIAN
She's got a job coming up for eight grand in a week. Can
you get me that?

LEON

Watch out for that cunt, though. She'll sell you out. She's not happy with you.

JULIAN
(*ironic*)
But you really care about me?

LEON

You walk a thin line, Julie. I wouldn't want to be in your shoes. You're getting awfully cocky. All the other boys are happy to have a car, a house in the hills. But not you, Julie. You got all your rich cunts lined up. Once-a-month tricks. A little tennis, an orgasm, a dip in the pool. But I'll warn you as a friend: if those cunts ever turn on you, you're through.

JULIAN

You sure?

LEON

They'll cut you out.

JULIAN
(*smiles*)
There's always gonna be more women, Leon.

Leon nods and smiles: ain't that the truth.

CUT TO:

INT. JULIAN'S APARTMENT — NIGHT

His digital clock reads 12.05; Julian is dressing to go out.

Nude from the waist up, he stands in front of the mirror. He unfolds a freshly laundered shirt and holds it to the mirror. He places an assortment of shirts, ties, sweaters, and belts on the bed, trying to decide which outfit will be right for tonight. This shirt with this belt? This belt with that tie?

The Miracles' 'The Love I Saw in You Was Just a Mirage' plays on the stereo. He starts to dress.

Playing two characters, he speaks to himself as he dresses. One character, amiable and outgoing, asks the questions; another, reserved and paranoid, answers them.

> JULIAN
>
> *Ar detta Ert forsta besok?*
>> *(beat)*
>
> *Nej, vivar har i fjol ocksa.*
>> *(beat)*
>
> *Ar Ni har ensam?*
>> *(beat)*
>
> *Jag ar har med mid min fru nagra vanner.*
>> *(beat)*
>
> *Far jag bjunda . . .*

The phone rings.

> *. . . pa en drink?*

Julian picks up the receiver.

> Yeah.
>> *(beat)*
>
> She says she's a friend?
>> *(beat)*
>
> Where does she know me from?
>> *(pause)*
>
> OK, let her come up.

He hangs up receiver. Julian checks his appearance in the mirror. The doorbell rings.

He answers the doorbell: Michelle stands in the doorway.

> MICHELLE
>
> I'm . . .

> JULIAN
>
> *Bonsoir.*

> MICHELLE
>
> . . . Michelle . . .

JULIAN

How did you find me?

Julian's reaction is polite, cold.

MICHELLE

It wasn't hard.
            (*walks in*)
Are you surprised?

JULIAN
            (*nothing surprises him*)
What do you want?

Michelle looks around the apartment. She's putting up a tough front.

MICHELLE

I would have thought you'd live in a place with soft lights, thick carpet, big circular bed, mirrors on the wall – you know, that sort of thing.

JULIAN

This is my apartment. Women don't come here.

MICHELLE

Oh.

There is an awkward pause. Michelle walks a few steps.

Are you going out?

JULIAN

Yeah.

MICHELLE

Business?

JULIAN

Maybe.

MICHELLE

Isn't it a little late?

JULIAN

Isn't it a little late for you?

MICHELLE

My husband's still in New York. I'm alone.

Julian lets her words hang in the air. He continues to make it uncomfortable for you.

Michelle musters her courage.

I thought it would be easier.

JULIAN

What?

MICHELLE

To 'be' with you. To procure you.

JULIAN

I told you you were mistaken. I don't do that.

Michelle's composure starts to slip. Her hands are shaking.

MICHELLE

Why are you doing this to me?

JULIAN

Doing what?

Michelle's lips quiver. She thought she could bluff her way through this – but now she is mortified, immobilized. She wishes she hadn't come.

MICHELLE

Embarrassing me.
                (*her voice trembles*)
I can't keep up this front much longer. I found out who you were. I looked you up. I came here in the middle of the night. I'm all alone. I wanted to know what it would be like. I want to fuck you. I brought money. What more can I do? Why do you humiliate me so?

Julian closes the door, shuts off the lights, and steps over to Michelle.

He smiles at her tenderly.

And starts to unbutton her blouse.

CUT TO:

INT. JULIAN'S BEDROOM — MORNING

Julian is on the phone; Michelle sleeps by his side. The telephone rests on a stack of books: Collectors' Guide to Antiques, Classic Furniture, Meubles français du XIIIe siècle, *and a Sotheby Parke Bernet catalogue.*

JULIAN

Oh, don't say that. You're getting me aroused just thinking about it. I'm lying here getting a hard-on and it's not even ten o'clock yet.

(*beat*)

Oh, now you're just teasing me. Stop talking like that or I'll have to hang up and jerk off right now.

(*beat*)

You like that, don't you?

Michelle wakes up listening to him.

Oh, baby, how can you say that? We're lying here talking about getting aroused and having more pleasure than you've had in ten years and you have to bring up some goddamn $800 stereo. How much is your husband worth? A couple million dollars? Of course I can do without it. I'll listen to the radio. I'll listen to your stereo.

(*beat*)

Lisa, Lisa, just listen to yourself. How can you say that?

He notices Michelle.

Can you hold a second? There's somebody at the door.

Julian puts his client on hold and turns to Michelle. He speaks to her as if she's the only person he's been thinking about.

Good morning.

(*polite kiss*)
What would you like for breakfast?

Michelle is taken aback by his chameleon-like changes.

MICHELLE

Well, ah . . .

JULIAN

Coffee, orange juice, eggs, croissant?

MICHELLE

Sure. No eggs.

Julian gets another line and dials room service.

JULIAN

This is Julian Kay. Two coffee, orange juice, croissant –
and one scrambled egg with a side of cottage cheese.

He reconnects himself with his client.

I'm sorry, Lisa, this is really embarrassing. There are some
people here and I have to hang up.
(*beat*)
I'll pick you up at six. See you then, love.

*Julian shakes his head to himself and cradles the receiver. He turns
back to Michelle.*

So what do you think?

MICHELLE

About what?

JULIAN

Did you make the right decision to come last night? Was it
what you expected?

MICHELLE

No, it was like sleeping with a real person. I'm not used to
that.

JULIAN

Do you remember what you said last night?

MICHELLE

Yes.

CUT TO:

INT. JULIAN'S APARTMENT — MORNING

They finish breakfast in the sitting room. He is wearing trousers and a silk navy bathrobe. She's fully dressed. A folded newspaper rests under his coffee cup.

He places his napkin on his plate and stands. It's Michelle's cue to leave. He kisses her forehead.

MICHELLE

What do you do today?

JULIAN

I've got to go to the health club.

MICHELLE

And see your friend this evening?

Julian shrugs.

Michelle hesitates, then speaks.

I want to apologize, Julian.

JULIAN

For what?

MICHELLE

I realize I was probably rude and insulting when I came here, and you were very kind to me. I had a good time.

JULIAN

So did I.

MICHELLE

So I guess I learned a lesson.

He realizes she is liking him too much, and becomes colder.

> JULIAN

I was rude, too.

> MICHELLE

Do you remember what *you* said last night?

> JULIAN
> (*polite smile*)

Yeah.

> MICHELLE
> (*half-serious*)

Do you say that to all the women?

> JULIAN
> (*without emotion*)

Yeah.

Michelle is again taken aback: she's confused by his interior and exterior selves. Is everything he does an act?

> MICHELLE

But I was different, wasn't I?

> JULIAN

What do you mean?

> MICHELLE

You said women didn't come to your apartment, and then you asked me to stay overnight?

> JULIAN
> (*nods*)

That's true. You're different in another way, too.

> MICHELLE

You mean I'm young.

> JULIAN
> (*cold*)

No. The price. It was awfully cheap.

He opens the door for her.

MICHELLE

Well, I thought maybe we'd do this again sometime.

JULIAN
(*smiles*)

No. I'm afraid not. It was very nice meeting you, Michelle.
I hope things work out with your husband.

Michelle, hurt and confused, leaves.

Julian closes the door behind her and thinks a moment.

CUT TO:

EXT. SOTHEBY PARKE BERNET — EARLY EVENING

*Julian escorts Lisa Williams, an attractive woman aged about forty,
into the Beverly Boulevard offices.*

CUT TO:

INT. MAIN EXHIBITION HALL — EARLY EVENING

*About a hundred people mill about the large rectangular hall. The
room is filled with antique furniture and artifacts. Framed paintings
and frayed prayer rugs hang on the walls.*

*Each item for auction is listed by lot number. Potential buyers study
the various lots, comparing them to the catalogue picture and
description.*

*Tracking across the cluttered hall, one is amazed by the diversity
and beauty of the items up for auction: a marquetry-inlaid George
III armoire, a rose Art Nouveau armchair, two matching Tiffany
lamps, a portrait of the Van Dyck school, and so on.*

Voices drift in and out of the pre-auction crowd:

*– Three black-suited Japanese soberly debate a gilt-mounted Louis
XIV commode.*

*– A young girl in jeans and a sweater examines an elegant Sarouk
carpet.*

– Two aging gents discuss a nude portrait: 'It may be Clinton's face, but it certainly *isn't Clinton's body.'*

– Julian and Lisa examine a Jacobean chest of drawers. Julian pulls out a drawer and studies the dovetails while Lisa reads the catalogue:

LISA
. . . late seventeenth century, unrestored.
(*turning pages*)
It's estimated at 2,800 to 3,000.

JULIAN
(*holding drawer*)
Somebody started to work on it. My guess is that it'll go
for more than three grand. Thirty-five hundred at least.
It's a great piece, but not a great buy. At twenty-eight hundred, it's a great buy. What do you think?

LISA
It looks just perfect for the guest room, but . . .

JULIAN
(*looking around*)
There's a George III chest around here somewhere that
won't go for more than twelve hundred. No bargain, but a
good investment at least. And the lines are beautiful . . .

Lisa spots someone across the hall.

LISA
Uh-oh.

JULIAN
. . . actually that hideous Louis Quatorze commode will
probably be the best buy if the Japs don't bid up on it.

LISA
Do you see who I see?

*Lisa looks across the room at Mrs Sloan, a highborn and over-
dressed woman in her late seventies.*

JULIAN

Who is it?

LISA

Randolph Sloan's widow. A stockholder in Jim's company.

JULIAN

Is she still alive?

LISA

She'll make a beeline straight here.

JULIAN

There goes the Louis Quatorze commode.

LISA

What'll I do?

Julian affects a German homosexual accent.

JULIAN

Come, Lisa, let's vace the enemy bevore it vaces us.

Adding a faint homosexual bounce to his buttocks, Julian escorts Lisa toward Mrs Sloan.

Mrs Sloan eyes them suspiciously.

LISA

Lucille, how nice to see you. Are you buying or selling?

MRS SLOAN

Just looking.

She says this as she turns her eyes on Julian.

Julian plays his beard role to the hilt: his English is barely comprehensible through a swishy kraut accent.

JULIAN

Der es an exquisite Louis Quatorze commode auf der.

LISA
(*introducing*)

Lucille, this is Willem Shoenvelt. He's helping me redecorate the guest house.

JULIAN
(*broken English*)

Great hospitality, madam.

He extends his hand. His wrist collapses as Mrs Sloan touches it.

I like eure dress very much greatly. I think it vill be much in style next year.

LISA
(*reproving*)

Willem.

Julian 'accidently' knocks over a Sheraton chair with his foot. Reaching down to pick it up, he bumps into Mrs Sloan. She in turn bumps into a brass floor lamp.

JULIAN

Entschuldigen sie bitte. Entschul . . .

Begging a hundred forgivenesses, Julian grabs the lamp before it falls and sets it upright. Bystanders turn and look. Lisa feigns shock and relief.

Ich bedaure sehr. I do not know what . . .

Julian bumps a $10,000 Tiffany lamp with his elbow and sends it toward the floor. This time Lisa is genuinely aghast.

Verdammt!

Julian reaches down and, in a continuous motion, grabs the Tiffany lamp and replaces it on the table. He shamefacedly looks around to see if anyone has noticed: everyone has.

A Sotheby Parke Bernet representative walks quickly toward them. Mrs Sloan is mortified.

Entschuldigen sie bitte. Auf wiedersehen.

Mrs Sloan and Lisa watch as Julian hurriedly leaves. Lisa turns to Mrs Sloan and shrugs.

   CUT TO:

EXT. SOTHEBY PARKE BERNET — LATE AFTERNOON

Lisa and Julian double over the side of his Mercedes laughing.

                    JULIAN
   My God! Did you see her?

Lisa is laughing so hard tears come down her cheeks. She puts her arm around Julian.

Perhaps this is the secret of Julian's success more than anything else: he makes women happy.

   CUT TO:

EXT. WESTWOOD APARTMENT HOTEL — DAY

Julian, wearing cut-off jeans, sits by the small hotel pool, sunning and reading the LA Times. *A can of diet soda rests beside his chair.*

He folds the paper over and looks at the lower front page. A news story catches his interest.

The caption reads: 'WIFE OF LOCAL FINANCIER SLAIN IN PALM SPRINGS HOME.'

A one-column photo of Judy Rhyman is below the headline. Julian reads on.

The story carries over to page three. There's a two-column photo of the Rhyman Palm Springs house.

Michelle, wearing French jeans and a pullover, walks into the pool area and approaches Julian. He folds the paper and says:

                    JULIAN
   I wish your husband would come back.

                    MICHELLE
   He has.

JULIAN

Oh.

Michelle pulls up a lawn chair and sits alongside Julian.

MICHELLE

I can't stop thinking about you.

Julian looks at her a moment, then turns his eyes back to the still-blue pool.

Do you mind?

JULIAN

What have you been doing?

MICHELLE

When?

JULIAN

This morning.

MICHELLE

Driving around.
          (beat)
I drove to Anaheim, then to Long Beach. Then I came here.

JULIAN
          (pause)
I'm not part of your problems, Michelle. I'm not the solution to your problems.

MICHELLE

I brought money.

JULIAN

I won't take it.

MICHELLE

A hundred dollars?

Julian, pained, looks away. Michelle says almost pleadingly:

More? 500?

He looks at her sympathetically.

>   JULIAN
> No.

>   MICHELLE
> I'll buy you the stereo.

>   JULIAN
> I've got a stereo.

>   MICHELLE
> What then?

He stands.

>   JULIAN
> Let's go.

>   MICHELLE
> What?

Julian takes her hand.

>   JULIAN
> I don't want your money. Let's go to my room.

> CUT TO:

INT. JULIAN'S BEDROOM — DAY

Julian and Michelle are in bed. He fingers a small gold cross hanging on a chain from her neck.

>   MICHELLE
>   (*smiles*)
> Bulgari. You want it?

>   JULIAN
> No.

>   MICHELLE
> I want to know everything about you.

>   JULIAN
> Why?

MICHELLE

I don't know. It seems important.

JULIAN

We just made love, didn't we?

MICHELLE

Yes.

JULIAN

Then you know all there is to know.

MICHELLE

Don't be childish. Where are you from?

JULIAN

No. I'm not 'from' anywhere. I'm from this bed. Everything that's worth knowing about me you can learn from letting me make love to you.

MICHELLE

That's not true. Why do you fuck older women?

JULIAN

What's older?

MICHELLE

Forty. Fifty. Sixty.

JULIAN

They pay me.

MICHELLE

So would I. So would many of my friends. What's so great about older women?

JULIAN

I see 'younger' women.

MICHELLE

So?

JULIAN

I prefer older women.

MICHELLE

Why?

JULIAN

What's the use of bringing some high-schooler to climax?
Some teenager who gets wet in the movies and goes home
to masturbate? That's no challenge. It has no meaning.
The other day – the day I met you in the hotel – I was
with a woman, somebody's mother, whose husband never
cared for her, who hadn't had an orgasm for ten years, if
at all. She tried to lie, but I could tell. This woman hadn't
been climaxed in a long time. It took me three hours to
get her off. For a while I didn't think I'd be able to do it at
all. My jaw was sore the whole next day. I almost wished I
used vibrators . . .

MICHELLE

You don't?

JULIAN

Never. But, you see, when it was over, I had really done
something. Something worthwhile. Something only I
could have done. Who else would have cared enough to
do it right? Young girls bore me.

CUT TO:

INT. LAPD – DAY

*Glenn Rhyman, wearing a conservative suit, sits in the nondescript
office of Detective Jack Sunday.*

*Sunday, a stocky man in a rumpled suit, sips a styrofoam cup of
coffee. He's been doing this a long time.*

*He pulls a pair of handcuffs out of the desk, looks at them a second,
and places them on the desktop. Rhyman sinks his head into his
hands:*

RHYMAN

Oh, my God.

SUNDAY

These are not the handcuffs your wife was wearing when
she was killed, Mr Rhyman. We found them in the study.
We also found some paddles, dildos, you know what I'm
talking about.

*Rhyman is expressionless. He knows all too well what Sunday is talk-
ing about.*

Look, I don't care about your private sex life. It's no concern of the LAPD. However, the manner in which your
wife was assaulted suggests that the killer was – may have
once been a 'guest' at your home.

Rhyman, grief-stricken, looks away and sighs.

I'll try to keep what you say in confidence, but I will have
to have detailed information about you and your wife's sex
practices and what parties, if any, were involved.

CUT TO:

EXT. WESTWOOD APARTMENT HOTEL – DAY

An unmarked police car is parked in the drive.

CUT TO:

INT. WESTWOOD APARTMENT HOTEL LOBBY – DAY

*Julian is speaking with Jill, the young desk clerk, as Detective Sun-
day enters.*

SUNDAY
(*to Jill*)
Does Mr Julian Kay live here?

Jill looks at Julian.

(*shows shield*)
I'm Detective Sunday from the Homicide Bureau. I'd like
to ask some . . .

Julian furtively glances at Jill. He prefers to keep his private life private.

JULIAN

I was just walking into Westwood. Can we talk there?

Julian heads for the front door. Sunday joins him.

CUT TO:

EXT. WILSHIRE BOULEVARD — DAY

They cross the street and walk toward Mé Mé restaurant.

JULIAN

Do you know Sergeant Thomas? John Thomas? He's in Internal Affairs, a . . .

SUNDAY
(cutting him off)

I'm investigating the Rhyman murder from the Los Angeles end. Do you know the case?

JULIAN

Was it in the paper?

SUNDAY

Yeah.

JULIAN

In Palm Springs?

SUNDAY

Yeah.

JULIAN

I think I read about it.

SUNDAY

I'll bet you did.

CUT TO:

INT. MÉ MÉ — DAY

Julian and Sunday face each other across a table looking out on Wilshire Boulevard. A waitress brings two coffees.

Julian shakes a packet of Sweet'n'Low into his cup and stirs the coffee.

SUNDAY

What is it *exactly* that you do, Mr Kay?

JULIAN

Julian. I'm a translator and guide. Sometimes a chauffeur.

SUNDAY

What were you doing last night?

JULIAN

I went with a friend to a pre-auction viewing at Sotheby Parke Bernet, then we spent the evening together.

SUNDAY

She'll verify that?

JULIAN

Of course, but I think she'd prefer to remain anonymous.

SUNDAY

Of course.

JULIAN

Am I a suspect?

SUNDAY

No, but I think you'd better let us check out this alibi to be on the safe side. For your sake.

Julian doesn't answer.

Now, this work you were doing for the Rhymans – was this as a translator or a chauffeur?

Julian enjoys verbal fencing as much as Sunday. They're both good at it.

JULIAN

Neither. This was more of a personal matter.

SUNDAY

You were friends.

JULIAN

Not exactly.

SUNDAY

Well, what, exactly, did you do at the Rhymans?

JULIAN

Nothing special. Just chit-chat. I have a hard time remembering, you know. I meet a lot of people.

SUNDAY

I understand your problem. Let's see: you talked a bit, had a few drinks, and the next thing you knew you were on your way back to Los Angeles.

JULIAN

More or less.

SUNDAY
(getting tough)

Julian, I'm gonna take you in. We've got our own memory refresher course. I think you'd like it. You seem like a young man who wants to improve himself.

Julian backs off.

JULIAN

Look, Detective, I want to cooperate with the police in any way I can. But you must understand there are delicate matters involved. Things which may not fall under the exact letter of the law. Publicity is the last thing I want.

SUNDAY

I won't book you, Julian. Though I could. I won't take away your chauffeur's license, though I could do that too. I could even bring you up on a drug charge. In your profession with your contacts, that shouldn't be hard. But I won't do that either.
(hard)
Just tell me about the Rhymans.

                              JULIAN
                          (*thinks a moment*)
OK.

CUT TO:

INT. BEVERLY WILSHIRE — NIGHT

A political fund-raiser. Between seventy-five and a hundred contributors sit around tables, enjoying the standard regimen of lukewarm chicken, peas, and political speeches.

A banner above the platform proclaims: CALIFORNIA DEMOCRATS WELCOME 22ND DISTRICT SENATOR CHARLES STRATTON.

Julian, wearing a black gabardine suit with a gray wool vest and silk tie, sits next to Mrs Laudner, an overdressed dowager who reeks of wealth and patronage.

Standing behind the 'Beverly Hilton' podium, a Hollywood actor introduces 'Charles Stratton.'

Julian — a textbook of good manners — applauds politely.

Mrs Laudner, visibly uncomfortable, is bored by the whole business. She nudges Julian.

                          MRS LAUDNER
Do you follow California politics, Julian?

                              JULIAN
Not very much.

                          MRS LAUDNER
You're smart. They're all whores.

She pokes a lethargic fork at her uneaten food. Julian stops her.

                              JULIAN
Don't eat this stuff. We're going out later.

Julian motions for a waiter to pick up their plates.

Charles Stratton steps up to the podium to a round of applause. Handsome, young, and tanned, he is the quintessence of Californian success.

Mrs Laudner whispers behind her palm to Julian:

> MRS LAUDNER
> This guy's a real comer.

Later.

Julian and Mrs Laudner stand in the reception line.

Stratton and his lovely wife greet his supporters and constituents.

Julian looks up and recognizes Stratton's 'lovely wife': it is Michelle. A flicker of emotion crosses his face.

Julian and Mrs Laudner step up to Stratton and Michelle.

Senator Stratton recognizes Mrs Laudner instantly.

> STRATTON
> Mrs Laudner, how nice of you to come. It's always a
> pleasure to see you again.

> MRS LAUDNER
> It's bullshit, but I like it. Can we talk later?

> STRATTON
> Of course. Mrs Laudner, this is my wife, Michelle.

Michelle automatically stretches out her hand and greets Mrs Laudner.

Julian watches Michelle play her role: she bears little resemblance to the girl who has been seeing him. She seems more like a mannequin than a person, an attractive adjunct to a well-oiled political machine.

> MRS LAUDNER
> And this is Julian Kay.

Michelle's lips tremble when she sees him. Her eyes betray her affection. She retains her composure.

Julian deferentially greets the Senator and his lovely wife.

> JULIAN
> My honor, Senator. Mrs Stratton.

(*looks at Michelle*)
You're a fortunate man, Senator.

After Julian and Mrs Laudner move forward with the line, Stratton leans over and whispers to Michelle.

STRATTON
You know what he is?

She watches Julian and Mrs Laudner walk away.

Crossing the room, Mrs Laudner turns to Julian and remarks:

MRS LAUDNER
That boy's gonna go far.
(*beat*)
And he's got a nice wife too.

Julian takes Mrs Laudner by the arm.

JULIAN
Tell me about them, Emily.

MRS LAUDNER
I said he was a comer.

JULIAN
No, about *them*. As a couple. What's their marriage like?

Julian speaks from genuine concern for Michelle. But Mrs Laudner thinks he's trying to set up another mark.

MRS LAUDNER
(*playful*)
Oh, Julian. You're incorrigible.

JULIAN
C'mon.

MRS LAUDNER
(*confidential*)
Well, it's no secret she's very unhappy.

CUT TO:

EXT. WESTWOOD BOULEVARD — DAY

The usual Westwood mix: stores, students, sun.

Julian, book in hand, walks south on Westwood. He watches his reflection in the store windows as he passes.

He turns into Tower Records.

    CUT TO:

INT. TOWER RECORDS

Julian, standing amid a gaggle of high-school girls, looks over the new album releases.

We continue to watch him from the observer's point of view. From the sidewalk, then from inside the store.

Julian turns: he is about to bump into us. Then he turns again, and moves down another aisle. We follow down a parallel aisle.

Then he abruptly turns toward us and looks up. He runs into the person who has been following him and smiles.

Michelle pretends to be looking through a record rack.

                    JULIAN
Hello there.

                    MICHELLE
                 (*feigns surprise*)
Oh. Hello, Julian.

                    JULIAN
You shop here often?

                    MICHELLE
Just browsing.

                    JULIAN
Me too.
                    (*gestures*)
Well, I've got to go. Nice to talk to you, Mrs Stratton.

Julian is teasing. He also wanted to 'bump' into her.

> MICHELLE

Wait.

Julian turns and walks back to her.

> I have to talk to you. Why don't we have a drink?

> JULIAN
> (*touches her hand*)

I'd like that. Now or later?

CUT TO:

INT. MOULING RESTAURANT

Julian and Michelle sit in a darkened nook in the bar section. She sips a whisky sour. He straightens her collar.

> MICHELLE

I wish you hadn't been there last night. I didn't want you to know who I was – am.

> JULIAN

It doesn't matter.

> MICHELLE

Jost is my maiden name.

> JULIAN

I've seen your husband on television. He's very impressive.

> MICHELLE

He's very ambitious.

> JULIAN

You should not see me any more. It only makes things worse for you.

> MICHELLE

Are you refusing to see me again?

Julian squeezes a lemon slice into his iced tea.

JULIAN
(*ironic*)

You looked quite nice in the reception line last night. Very
demure and proper.

MICHELLE

What is that supposed to mean?

JULIAN

Nothing.

*Cautious and afraid, they toy with each other. Julian and Michelle
are moving together emotionally, but neither wants to be the first to
admit it.*

MICHELLE

I would never do anything to hurt him politically. I could
never leave him. I would die first.

JULIAN

You're dying now. You're becoming a non-person. Another
five years and there'll be nothing left.

MICHELLE

Why are you saying this to me?

JULIAN

Because I know you. I understand you. I can help you.

MICHELLE
(*in awe*)

Boy, you're really good. You've really got that bullshit
down pat.

JULIAN

Don't let your husband blackmail you.

MICHELLE

He has this big political thing about having a wife and
family. He keeps wanting me to get pregnant.

JULIAN

Who are we talking about? You or him?

                              MICHELLE
I can't tell any more.
                          (*almost desperate*)
What can I do?

                              JULIAN
I don't know: be yourself?

                              MICHELLE
Leave him?

                              JULIAN
His career will survive. People forget. These things have to
be done quietly. Don't let him fool you with his talk about
duty and self-sacrifice. He's getting what he wants. You
have to do the same: take the pleasure when you can.

She sips her empty glass.

                              MICHELLE
And you, Julian? Where do you come in? Where do you
get pleasure?

CUT TO:

INT. WESTWOOD APARTMENT HOTEL — DAY

Jill calls Julian over as he enters.

                               JILL
Julian.

                              JULIAN
                          (*walks over*)
Hey, Jill.

                               JILL
There was a kid here looking for you.

                              JULIAN
                          (*suspicious*)
What did he want?

JILL

He wouldn't say. He seemed to know where your room
was. I told him he couldn't go up and he left.

JULIAN

Black or white?

JILL

White. About eighteen. Blond hair.

JULIAN

What was he wearing?

JILL

Jeans, tennis shoes, white shirt. Is anything wrong?

He dismisses her concerns with a wave of his hand.

JULIAN

No. Thanks for telling me. See you later.

Thinking to himself, Julian heads toward his room.

CUT TO:

EXT. BEVERLY WILSHIRE HOTEL — DAY

A Beverly Hills landmark.

CUT TO:

INT. EL PADRINO ROOM — DAY

*The late afternoon crowd is sprinkled with members of Julian's
native class: the young, the beautiful, the rich, and the deeply
tanned.*

*Julian and Lillian, an attractive mid-fortyish woman, sit in an out-
of-the-way booth. Julian's copy of* The Uses of Enchantment *rests
beside her arm.*

LILLIAN
(*looks at book*)
This was really thoughtful of you, Julian.

JULIAN

It's quite a good book. I thought you'd like it.

LILLIAN

I'll read it.

JULIAN

Then we can . . .

LILLIAN
(*secretive*)

You know what I *really* would like, Julian?

JULIAN
(*inviting*)

No, what?

LILLIAN

I'm embarrassed to say.

JULIAN

C'mon, Lillian, there's no secrets between us.

LILLIAN

Well, there's this kid who does our lawn, you know. A
Spanish boy. He must only be seventeen. I just sit in the
kitchen and watch him. I can't take my eyes off him. I fan-
tasize about him coming into the bedroom, taking off his
jeans . . .

JULIAN

He works alone?

LILLIAN

His father leaves after about an hour, then he's the only
one here.

JULIAN

What are you afraid of, Lillian? You surprise me. You're a
good-looking woman. Just because you're not some silly little schoolgirl, you think you're not allowed to desire young
men? How foolish you are. You're a good-looking woman,
but you're afraid, you're embarrassed of being yourself.

(*beat*)

Don't disappoint me, Lillian. Next time he comes by and it's hot out and he's sweating, ask him in for a Coke. He'll appreciate it. His other employers don't pay any attention to him. They think he's just some dumb spic kid. Be nice to him.

CUT TO:

INT. BEVERLY WILSHIRE LOBBY — DAY

Julian, straightening his coat, walks out of the El Padrino room, through the lobby and into the barbershop.

CUT TO:

INT. BARBERSHOP — DAY

Julian sits in one of the chairs and motions to the bootblack.

JULIAN

Joe.

BOOTBLACK

Just a second, Mr Kay.

Detective Sunday walks into the barbershop, looks around, spots Julian. He walks over.

SUNDAY

What a surprise. Mr Kay.

JULIAN
(*suspicious*)

Yeah, there've been quite a few coincidences lately. It's getting to be a pattern.
(*beat*)

Sit down, Detective. Get a shine. You need it. On me.

SUNDAY

Thank you, Julian.

Sunday looks at his scruffy shoes and sits next to Julian. The boot-

black brings his stool over and starts to shine Julian's brown Armanis.

You're quite dressed up today.

JULIAN

I have to go over to the Country Club.

SUNDAY

We checked out your alibi. Mrs Williams says she was with you Tuesday night, but that you dropped her off at seven. The Rhyman murder was at ten.

JULIAN

Shit.

(*beat*)

But I described her house. Her bedroom.

SUNDAY

She said that you had been helping her redecorate. That you had been to Parke Bernet looking for a bureau.

(*beat*)

I can understand why she might say that. She has a reputation to protect.

Julian, shaking his head to himself, is more piqued than surprised: 'Does it just figure?'

Sunday, studying Julian's reactions, mixes his 'hard' and 'soft' questions.

(*pleasantly curious*)

How do you do it, Julian? This afternoon with Mrs Jarvie, tonight at the Country Club. How do you seduce all these women?

Julian looks at Sunday coldly. The Detective has been fucking with his client list: interrogating Mrs Williams, spying on Mrs Jarvie. With attention like this, Julian will soon be back out on the streets.

JULIAN

I'll tell you what, Sunday. You've been bugging me quite a bit. Spying on me, digging into my private life. You ease

off my clients a bit and I'll tell you how to get more
women.

SUNDAY

How's that?

The bootblack moves over to Sunday's chair.

JULIAN

First, obviously, you dress for shit. But anybody can fix
that. It's your face. And your body. You carry yourself all
wrong. You got back problems? And your jaw . . .
(*gestures*)
. . . it hangs so loose. Tighten it up a little. Do some jaw
exercises . . .

SUNDAY

Doesn't it ever bother you, Julian?

JULIAN

What?

SUNDAY

What you do.

JULIAN

Giving women pleasure? I should feel guilty about that?

SUNDAY

But it's not legal.

JULIAN

But legal is not always right. Men make the laws, and
sometimes men are wrong. Or stupid. Or jealous.

SUNDAY

And you know better?

JULIAN

There are men who are above the law.

SUNDAY

How do these men know who they are?

                              JULIAN

They know.

                              (*beat*)

They ask themselves.

                              SUNDAY

Why didn't you tell me you handcuffed Mrs Rhyman?

                              JULIAN

I didn't.

                              SUNDAY

Yeah, you said that. That's why I went back and checked it
twice with the coroner. Mrs Rhyman's wrists were cut up
quite a bit where the cuffs were – apparently she put up
quite a fight after she was handcuffed. But, underneath
the cuts . . .

                              (*gestures*)

. . . there were bruises from where she had been cuffed
earlier. The coroner estimates about forty-eight hours earlier. Which would be the night you were there.

Julian is silent. The bootblack finishes Sunday's shoes.

                              JULIAN

I'll take care of you in a minute, Joe.

*Joe walks off. Sunday takes a black-and-white 5 by 7 out of his
pocket and hands it to Julian: it is a grisly crime-scene photo of
Judy Rhyman's body.*

                              SUNDAY

She was beaten with a heavy metal object, raped, then vio-
lated with an object – presumably the murder weapon.

Julian pales when he sees the photograph.

                              JULIAN

Jesus Christ.

He tries to explain.

    Yeah, I handcuffed her, but you've got to understand

people like the Rhymans. It's like a game to them. I'll
explain . . .

Sunday listens.

CUT TO:

EXT. WESTWOOD APARTMENT HOTEL STAIRS — DAY

Julian walks through the lobby. He is suspicious and angry.

His fears are confirmed. Jill says as he passes the desk:

> JILL
> They were here two hours. I couldn't stop them. They had
> a search warrant.

Julian heads upstairs.

CUT TO:

INT. JULIAN'S ROOM — DAY

*Julian's suite is a mess. The police have searched every corner: the
mattress has been pulled off its springs, books off the shelves, drawers
out of the dresser. After a moment, Julian picks up the receiver and
dials.*

> JULIAN
> Hi, Jill. It's Julian. You can send the maid in now.

He hangs up and looks around the room.

CUT TO:

EXT. ANNE'S HOUSE — DAY

Julian's car is parked outside.

CUT TO:

INT. ANNE'S HOUSE — DAY

Julian walks into the empty house.

Anne, sitting on the deck, sees him and walks over. She wears shorts and a Hermes T-shirt.

Tim, a boy aged about seven, bounces a beach ball on the sun deck.

> ANNE
>
> You're becoming a regular visitor, Julian. What's happening?

> JULIAN
>
> Something I wanted to talk about.

Anne motions toward the boy.

> ANNE
>
> I don't like to have anybody in the house when Tim visits. The courts might not let me see him at all.

> JULIAN
>
> Let's go to the beach.

CUT TO:

EXT. MALIBU BEACH — DAY

Julian and Anne walk along the beach.

> JULIAN
>
> I think I'm in a frame.

> ANNE
>
> Who's putting you in?

> JULIAN
>
> I'm not sure. I can only see the frame.
> (*beat*)
> It's the Rhyman murder. You know, in Palm Springs.

A teenage girl and her water-soaked Irish Setter dash down the beach past them.

> ANNE
>
> You tricked with them?

JULIAN

Only once. As a favor to Leon.

ANNE
(*without emotion*)

You two-timing bastard.

JULIAN

So I'm a nice guy. I can't help it. Would you ask around?

ANNE

Why don't you ask your new friend Leon?

JULIAN

I may just do that.

ANNE

You trick for other people. You cheat me out of money. Then, when you need a favor, you come back to me.

Julian looks out across the ocean.

If I help you, you'll have to help me.

JULIAN

How?

ANNE

You'll have to come back to me. Work strictly for me.

JULIAN

That doesn't have anything to do with this.

ANNE

Like shit it doesn't. When I found you, you were on the street sucking cock. I taught you how to treat women. How to make love. Then one day you come to me and say, 'I'm too good for you,' and cut me out. It ain't right, Julie.

JULIAN

It's different now, Anne. I'm more than I used to be. When I'm good now, I don't even have to make love. I'm getting older. I've got to move forward.

ANNE

Please, Julie, save me the speeches.
(*pause*)
How's the Swedish coming?

JULIAN

I'll be ready.

ANNE

She's coming in a week from today.

JULIAN

What do they want?

ANNE

Chauffeur, guide, part-time translator. She apparently has
certain sexual idiosyncrasies. She's wired to a lot of auto
money.
(*beat*)
You gonna come back with me?

Julian nods. They continue down the beach.

You did it, didn't you?

JULIAN

What?

ANNE

The Rhyman killing.

He doesn't answer.

Don't worry, Julie. It doesn't matter.

Julian looks out back across the ocean: a vast, empty plain.

CUT TO:

INT. JULIAN'S ROOM — DAY

*Julian, barefooted, wearing jeans and an 'Ohio U' T-shirt, holds a
ten-pound dumb-bell in hand. He alternates between curls and
high–low arm lifts.*

The Berlitz cassette is on the player. Julian speaks to the mirror as he lifts the weights.

> CASSETTE
> *Hur lange behover jag vanta?*
> > (*beat*)
> How long must I wait?

> JULIAN
> *Hur lange behover jag vanta?*
> > (*beat*)
> How long must I wait?

The cassette runs out. Julian continues his arm curls. He repeats the last line, placing the emphasis on a different word each time. Each line has a different meaning.

> How *long* must I wait?
> > (*beat*)
> How long must *I* wait?
> > (*beat*)
> How long must I *wait*?

> CUT TO:

EXT. BEL AIR HOME — DAY

Julian climbs out of his Mercedes and walks across the leisurely green lawn of a Bel Air estate.

A seventeen-year-old Spanish youth clips the hedge as his father runs a power mower across the lawn.

Julian steps over to the Spanish youth:

> JULIAN
> *Hola. Habla usted inglés?*

> SPANISH YOUTH
> *Un poco.*

> JULIAN
> *Quiere usted ayudarme? Estoy buscando por 890 North . . .*
> > (*looks at him closely*)

. . . you work for Mrs Jarvie, don't you? She has a house in
Brentwood. On Carmelina just north of Sunset.

> SPANISH YOUTH
> (*thinks*)

Si. We work there.

> JULIAN
> (*digressing*)

I really shouldn't tell you this, but I was at her house last
week and we were sitting in the kitchen and she was talking about you.

The youth grins sheepishly.

> SPANISH YOUTH

No?

> JULIAN

She's really a nice woman, a good-looking woman. You
should meet her some time. She's kind. I like her a lot.
> (*confidential*)

You should knock on the door. Say hello. I think she
would like to meet you. She's . . .
> (*shrugs*)

. . . well, just forget I said anything.

*The Spanish youth's father looks over reprovingly, but the youth dis-
misses his critical glare with a wave of his hand: don't worry, it's all
right, Dad.*

CUT TO:

EXT. GOLDWATER CANYON — DAY

Julian's Mercedes winds its way up the canyon.

CUT TO:

EXT. WILLIAMS HOUSE

*Julian pulls into the driveway of a Coldwater Canyon home and
gets out.*

He presses a wrinkle out of his trousers and rings the doorbell. A maid answers:

MAID

Yes?

JULIAN

I'd like to speak to Mrs Williams. My name is Julian Kay.

MAID

Just a moment.

Julian nervously waits. A moment later, Lisa Williams comes to the door.

LISA
(*defensive*)

Hello, Julian. Why are you here?

JULIAN

Can I talk to you?

LISA

What do you want?

Julian tries to edge his way inside. Lisa holds her ground.

JULIAN

Have the police talked to you?

LISA

Yes, there was a detective here. I was very surprised you used my name.

JULIAN

I'm very, very sorry about that, Lisa, but this is very important. This is my life.

Lisa struggles to maintain her front.

LISA

I told the detective the truth.

JULIAN

But I was here, Lisa, I was here with you until midnight.

LISA

Julian, that's not . . . I can't. You weren't here.

A casually dressed, middle-aged man, Jim Williams, walks to the door and stands beside his wife.

WILLIAMS

What is it, dear?

LISA

This is Julian Kay. The boy who was helping with the decorating. The one who told the police he was with me the night of that murder.

Williams eyes Julian with cold disdain.

WILLIAMS

It's bad enough you make a fool of my wife at Parke Bernet, but then you go spreading your dirty lies. Leave us alone.

JULIAN

I swear, Mr Williams, I'm not lying.

Williams edges Lisa behind him. He is in control here, not his wife.

WILLIAMS
(*hateful*)

I don't know what you did. I don't want to know. Whatever it is, you're going to have to pay for it. And you're not going to get out of it by dragging me or my wife into your sordid affairs.

JULIAN

The truth. That's all I'm asking for.

WILLIAMS

I know you're lying.

JULIAN

How?

Williams looks him straight in the eye.

WILLIAMS
Because I was here with my wife the entire evening.

CUT TO:

INT. JULIAN'S ROOM — NIGHT

Julian and Michelle, both clothed, sit cross-legged on his large bed.

MICHELLE
Thank you, it's been a wonderful evening.

JULIAN
Tack, det har varit en underbar kvall.

After each response, they move closer to each other.

MICHELLE
Can I see you again tomorrow?

JULIAN
Kan vi traffas imorgon?

Michelle whispers seductively.

MICHELLE
Do you live alone?

JULIAN
Bor Ni ensam?

Michelle slips into French:

MICHELLE
Je crois que je t'aime beaucoup.

JULIAN
Moi aussi.

They embrace and roll on the bed together. Their tongues are lost in each other's mouths.

Julian runs his hand down her firm leg. She grasps his buttocks.

He unsnaps her jeans and starts to unzip her fly.

MICHELLE

No, not yet.

Julian pulls her zipper down.

JULIAN

Huh?

MICHELLE

Please, Julian, I don't want to fuck yet.

JULIAN
(*confused*)

Why not?

MICHELLE

Let's just make out some more.

He pulls back from her embrace.

JULIAN

What's wrong?

MICHELLE
(*kissing him*)

I just want to make out some more.

Julian, baffled, pushes her back.

JULIAN

Michelle. You love to make love. What's wrong?

MICHELLE

I love to be with you, to talk to you. I love it when you kiss
me, when you touch me . . . but not when you fuck me.
Because when you fuck me you go to work.

JULIAN

But you loved to make love before.

She zips up her fly.

MICHELLE

That was before.

JULIAN

Before what?

MICHELLE

Before I cared about you.

JULIAN

If it's your period, that's all right with me. In fact, I like
the taste of the blood, I love the . . .

MICHELLE
(*cuts him short*)

Don't give me that bullshit. You know what I'm talking
about. I can't give you any pleasure. You can't fool me: I see
the way you dramatize your 'orgasm' just to give me pleasure. Such a big production, but you really hold yourself
above everything. Always at a distance, always in control.

JULIAN

But I get my pleasure from pleasing you.

MICHELLE

That's not enough – not for you, not for me. I can't take
sex unless I can give it – and there's nothing you will take
from me.

JULIAN

You don't know what you're talking about.

MICHELLE

Yes I do. And so do you.

*Julian stands and walks over to the stereo. He fools around with a
couple of tapes but can't seem to get one into the tape deck.*

JULIAN

Yeah, I do. You're talking about me changing my life.
About giving up what I do.

MICHELLE

Is that so shocking?

JULIAN

What do you want me to say? That I care about you? All
right, damnit, I care. I really do.

MICHELLE

It's still not enough.

*Julian walks over to his portable typewriter and looks at the half-
written page in the carriage: it's a letter to the Manager of the Westwood Apartment Hotel on Los Angeles Police Department
stationery.*

JULIAN

How can I quit? This is all I'm good at . . .

MICHELLE

That's not true.

JULIAN
(*pause*)
Besides, I can't quit. I need the protection.

MICHELLE

What protection?

JULIAN

The people I know take care of each other. If I quit, I'd be
out on a limb.

MICHELLE

Then we'd be even. I'm already out on one.

JULIAN

I'm in trouble right now. I need their help.

Michelle doesn't understand.

I'm being framed by somebody. I don't know who. There
was a murder in Palm Springs a couple weeks ago. The
police think I did it. It was a woman I met once, but I was
some place else. But my alibi completely denies it.

MICHELLE
(*astonished*)
Why would anyone want to do that to you?

JULIAN
That's what I can't figure out. It doesn't make any sense.

MICHELLE
When was the murder?

JULIAN
A week ago Tuesday.

He sits on the bed next to Michelle.

MICHELLE
Weren't we together that night?

JULIAN
(*looks in her eyes*)
Baby, I wish we were.

He puts his arms around her and kisses her passionately. She starts to pull back. He kisses her neck.

All right, we won't make love.

CUT TO:

EXT. WESTWOOD — DAY

Julian is again walking through Westwood. He is again being followed. We see him from an unseen observer's point of view.

He walks up Westwood and turns on Weyburn. He stops and glances at clothes in a men's store window. He is aware that he is being followed.

Walking on, he glances back and sees who is tracking him: a young man in his mid-twenties.

Julian's eyes flit forward and back again.

Watching his follower's reaction in a store window, Julian cuts across the street. Floyd, the young man, follows.

Passing the Hamburger Hamlet, Julian cuts through the entrance to the Bruin Theater.

He ducks behind a corner and waits. When Floyd turns the corner, Julian grabs him by the collar and smashes him against one of the movie-poster display windows and frisks him.

JULIAN

You're really not very good at this, you know.

The young man is frightened and nervous. He's obviously had no previous experience as a gumshoe.

FLOYD

What?

JULIAN

Following people. You're lousy at it.

FLOYD

Who are you? What are you talking about?

JULIAN

Who's paying you? You're too obvious to be a cop. Leon?

FLOYD

I'm going to call the police.

Julian reaches into the young man's jacket and removes his wallet.

JULIAN

Go ahead.

Julian flips through the wallet pulling out credit cards and other pieces of identification.

Let's see: Floyd Wicker, BankAmericard, Master Charge, driver's license . . .

FLOYD
(*grabbing*)

Give those back.

JULIAN
(*pushes him away*)
. . . born 7-23-52. 1405 North Hawthorne, LA 90046. Picture of girlfriend: so-so. Her eyes are too close together. American Express. State Congressional Library pass . . .
(*getting interested*)
State of California employee identification, Senate pass, Charles Stratton, California . . .
(*angry*)
Who the fuck are you?

The young man grabs his wallet and cards back.

FLOYD
You can read, can't you?

JULIAN
You work for Senator Charles Stratton?

FLOYD
(*shrugs*)
Yeah.

JULIAN
Why are you following me?

FLOYD
I was told to.

JULIAN
By the Senator?

FLOYD
Who else?

JULIAN
Why?

FLOYD
I was really following his wife. But that led to you.

JULIAN
How long have you worked for Stratton, Floyd?

                         FLOYD
Six months.

                         JULIAN
Jesus Christ. And this guy wants to run for Congress.

                         FLOYD
He didn't think it would be right to hire a private detective.

                         JULIAN
What do you know about me?

                         FLOYD
You're just a guy who's been seeing his wife – or vice versa.

                         JULIAN
If the Senator wants to know about my private life, why doesn't he ask me himself?

The young man doesn't answer. Julian fumbles in the pocket of his khaki jacket and pulls out a felt pen.

Holding Floyd's face with one hand, Julian writes bold black numerals across his head: 636-1636.

Here, Floyd, this is my phone number. Just so you won't forget. If Stratton wants to talk to me, just have him call.
                    (*pushes him away*)
Now leave me alone.

The young man, embarrassed, touches his forehead and walks out of the Bruin Theater entrance.

Julian watches him for a moment, then heads in the opposite direction.

    CUT TO:

EXT. WILSHIRE BOULEVARD – NIGHT

A discreet sign indicates the LOS ANGELES COUNTRY CLUB.

EXT. LA COUNTRY CLUB — NIGHT

Julian sits on the patio.

The Country Club looms behind him like an antebellum mansion. Blacks and Filipinos, dressed as waiters, collect and deliver drink orders. The women wear skirts; the men jackets and ties. The children, like miniature versions of their parents, sit soberly and try to look respectable.

The patio overlooks a fountain and the ninth hole. In the distance, above the fir trees, one can see the lights of Trousdale and the Hollywood Hills.

The WASP Holy of Holies.

Julian sips his bourbon Manhattan, looks at the door, and waits.

Senator Stratton, an assistant, and Floyd (with traces of felt pen on his forehead) appear at the door. The young man says something to Stratton and points out Julian. The assistant gives the maître d' *a tip.*

Stratton walks over to Julian. The assistant and Floyd find another table.

Julian watches the Senator out of the corner of his eye, then goes back to his Manhattan.

Stratton pulls up a white wrought-iron chair and sits down across the table. Julian shows no emotion.

> STRATTON
> I received your message, Mr Kay. I thought I'd come see you in person.

A black waiter promptly arrives tableside.

> Vodka tonic, please.

Julian waits for the waiter to leave.

> JULIAN
> This is a surprise, Senator. I'm happy to see you haven't lost touch with your constituency.

STRATTON

I'm not talking as a Senator now, I'm talking as a husband.

JULIAN

That's too bad. I'm not a wife.

STRATTON

What do you want?

JULIAN

Want?

STRATTON

I know who you are. I've had you researched. I can't stop
my wife from being a fool, but I can stop her from being
blackmailed.

Julian glances back at the door. He's expecting someone.

JULIAN

I don't know what you're talking about.

STRATTON

You don't? A week ago you murdered a woman in Palm
Springs. I won't bother with the niceties of presumed
innocence. Three days later you saw my wife at a fund-
raiser and seduced her. You think you can blackmail me
into helping you.

*As Stratton speaks, an overdressed fiftyish woman walks in, spots
Julian, smiles and walks toward him. Then she sees Stratton and
abruptly turns on her heel and exits.*

JULIAN
(*watching her go*)

You're crazy.

STRATTON

Am I? My wife asked me last night about the Rhyman murder. It didn't make any sense until I heard about you . . .

JULIAN
(*interrupting*)
Have you discussed this with Michelle?

With just one look, Julian knows Stratton has not confided in his wife. This kind of man doesn't confide in anyone.

STRATTON
(*ignoring Julian's question*)
. . . You won't blackmail me. You can threaten to spread our names over every tabloid, but I won't interfere with the legal process.

The waiter brings Stratton's vodka tonic. They wait for him to leave.

JULIAN
You don't know what the fuck you're talking about, mister.

STRATTON
I know a whore when I see one. How much?

Julian looks Stratton in the eye and realizes how much he hates him.

JULIAN
Not to see your wife again?

Stratton nods.

Two grand.

STRATTON
You got a deal. I don't want to give you a check. I'll get you the cash in about an hour.

Julian points at Stratton.

JULIAN
I'm seeing Michelle because I want to see her – and she wants to see me.
(*growing angry*)
I don't want a fucking dime from you. I was just testing

you, trying to see what kind of man you were. There ain't
no amount of money you got that I want.

Stratton responds to Julian's disdain in kind.

STRATTON
Let me be even simpler. You live off the good graces of a
small number of people – such as Mrs Andrews, who was
just at the door a minute ago.
(*gestures*)
And the good graces of places such as this. Before you
have time to stand up, I can have you barred from this
club. And Perino's. And Chasen's. Same goes for your
clients. You're just a hanger-on. And unless you want to
find another crowd to hang on to, you'd better not see my
wife again.

This gives Julian pause for thought.

CUT TO:

EXT. HOLLYWOOD – NIGHT

*Julian wheels his Mercedes around a corner and heads up Highland
Avenue. He removes his bow tie and loosens his collar.*

*He plugs a cassette into the stereo and turns east on Hollywood to
the hard-driving beat of the J. Geils Band: 'Struttin' with My
Baby.'*

*It's past midnight; the stores and restaurants are closed. The theater-
goers and tourists have gone home. The streets now belong to their
natural denizens: the hustlers, hookers, pimps, transvestites, and
omnipresent patrol cars.*

*Studying the sidewalks, he drives down Selma and turns back on
Highland.*

*Further down Highland: Julian walks out of the Paradise Ballroom,
lingering to talk to a couple of hustlers in the doorway. He walks
back to his Mercedes and drives off.*

He parks on Santa Monica Boulevard and walks downs the block

*toward The Probe. He brushes past a young man propped against
the doorway as he enters.*

CUT TO:

INT. THE PROBE — NIGHT

*Julian draws some scattered hostile stares. The Probe is a gay bar
which caters to the rougher street trade. The air hangs heavy with
passion and paranoia.*

*He looks out of place in his dinner jacket. The room is packed,
elbow-to-elbow, buttocks-to-buttocks, with short-haired young men
in jeans and T-shirts. Cowboys, hard-hats, leatherboys, telephone
repairmen — by night. By day, salesmen, copywriters, junior execu-
tives.*

*Julian taps a street kid on the shoulder and asks him a question.
The kid shrugs and walks off.*

*An aura of hostility surrounds Julian. He's not happy to be here —
and nobody's particularly happy to have him here. He's not well
thought of in the hustler crowd — he moved uptown and now he
thinks he's too good for them.*

*Julian looks around and spots Jason, an old acquaintance, and
elbows his way toward him.*

JASON
Well, Julian. I haven't seen you in a long time. What
brings . . .

JULIAN
(*cuts him short*)
I'm looking for Leon. I heard he might be here. Have you
seen him?

JASON
Yeah, he was here advertising his new boy. A cute little
blond kid. I think he's out back somewhere.

JULIAN
Thanks, Jason.

JASON
(*sarcastic*)

It was nice seeing you again.

Julian squeezes his way across the dance floor to the rear of the club where he finds Leon scrunched up against the wall. He sidles next to him.

LEON

Julie. I thought that was you. What is this? Homecoming?

JULIAN

I've been trying to find you.

LEON

Let's go out back where it's quieter.

CUT TO:

EXT. THE PROBE — NIGHT

Julian and Leon lean against the railing.

LEON

What are you doing here?

Julian shrugs.

JULIAN

I heard you were showing off a new boy.

LEON
(*nods and looks back*)

Gotta make sure one of these fruits don't steal him from me.

JULIAN

Have you heard anything about the Rhyman killing?

LEON

That's *all* I've been hearing about. Fuckin' cops been on my ass like glue.

JULIAN

I've been getting the third degree.

LEON

So have half the boys in town. You saw what it was like in there. Everybody's waiting for a crackdown.

JULIAN

I may need some help. I don't have an alibi. It was you that sent me there, you know.

LEON

You need one?

JULIAN

Yeah.

LEON

I'll see what I can do.

JULIAN

Who do you think killed her?

LEON
(*shrugs*)

If I was a cop I'd be more interested in Rhyman himself – he's a freak.

JULIAN

But he's got an alibi.

LEON

Big deal.
(*changing the subject*)
Hey, Julie, I got a thing later tonight I'll let you in on. Pocket money.

JULIAN

Straight?

LEON

This time of night? You're kidding.

Julian looks away. Two boys walk off.

JULIAN

I'm through doing your shit, Leon. Through with your
rough trade, your goddamn kinky numbers. That's all
over . . .

LEON

I heard about your other problems too.

JULIAN

What problems?

LEON

Your clients, Julie. Your rich pussy. They're looking for
new boys. The cops have made you too hot. They won't
touch you. Ask around . . .

JULIAN

Fuck 'em.

LEON

Hey, Julie, you ask me to help you out of a tight spot. I'm
glad to do it. But then you tell me you won't do my tricks.
How you expect me to help you?

Julian winces: he's caught again.

JULIAN
(*pause*)

You get me the alibi, then we'll talk about the tricks.

CUT TO:

EXT. BEVERLY HILLS — NIGHT

*Julian's 450 SL speeds down Santa Monica Boulevard. The streets
are deserted.*

CUT TO:

INT. STRATTON BEDROOM — NIGHT

*Michelle, wearing a pink bathrobe, sits on the kingsize bed. Charles
Stratton, barefoot in black trousers, stands by the curtained windows.*

Both look very tired. The tears have dried on Michelle's cheeks.

A console TV continues to glow, long after the station has signed off the air.

STRATTON

I didn't know you hated me that much.

MICHELLE

I don't hate you.

STRATTON

No?

MICHELLE
(*to herself*)

I don't hate you.

He pulls a shoe-tree out of a black wing-tip, shakes it aimlessly in the air, then replaces it and sets the shoe back on the dresser.

STRATTON

What else do you call it? Consideration? Affection? Other wives have 'nervous breakdowns' or go on long vacations, but you hire a male prostitute.

MICHELLE
(*wincing*)

Oh, my God, Charles, don't start again.

STRATTON

But you won't stop seeing him?

Michelle doesn't answer. Stratton steps over to the TV and flips the channel selector until he finds an all-night station.

MICHELLE

He needs me. He's all alone. He needs someone.

STRATTON

He! What about me? Are you going to be able to live with what you're doing to me? I'm losing my wife – who I love. I'm on the very brink of getting my party's nomination for Congress. Instead of getting that nomination, I'll become

the subject of slander, gossip. I'll be ridiculed, possibly
forced out of politics. Is that what you want to do to me?

> MICHELLE
> (*distraught*)

No, Charles, no.

> STRATTON

I'm going to step on him, you know. He's just a little bug
who's wandered too far out on the highway. And I've got
to squash him.

> MICHELLE

What can I do?

> STRATTON

To save him? Or to help me?

> MICHELLE

They're not the same. I care about you, it's just that I . . .

> STRATTON

Love him.
> (*resigned*)
I'll tell you what to do. Take a rest. Don't rush into anything. Go to Europe for several months. You're not feeling
well. Get some psychiatric help, have your affair over there
if you like. When you come back the primaries will be
over. We can face the problem then.
> (*beat*)

Please.

Michelle mulls this over. It's cruel, but it's the least she can do.

CUT TO:

EXT. WESTWOOD APARTMENT HOTEL — DAY

CUT TO:

INT. JULIAN'S ROOM — DAY

Julian opens the door: Michelle, tired and red-eyed, stands waiting.

She smiles through her exhaustion. She's happy to see him.

MICHELLE
Hello, Julian. I have to talk . . .

Emotion sweeps over Julian. His heart leaps out to hers. He pulls her body to his.

JULIAN
Michelle. I've been trying to find you. I wanted to see you.

Julian pulls back and looks at Michelle.

What's the matter, baby? You look completely worn out.

MICHELLE
I didn't get much sleep.

JULIAN
Let's take a walk. Let me put my shoes on.

CUT TO:

EXT. UCLA BOTANICAL GARDEN — DAY

They walk up Hilgard past LeConte and turn at the small sign reading 'UCLA Botanical Garden.'

Thirty yards from the street, the Botanical Garden is a world unto itself: a verdant jungle of exotic plants, imported trees, labyrinthine paths, and artificial brooks. Each specimen is labeled: the Japanese aralia, the Mexican fan palm, the hydrangeas.

JULIAN
(*hesitant*)
I've been thinking about what you said the other day. I know what you were talking about. You have to under-stand it's not easy for me. But I think . . .

Michelle can't let him continue.

MICHELLE
Don't go any further.

She stops and sits by a gnarled yucca tree. He sits beside her.

JULIAN

What do you mean?

MICHELLE

I can't bear to hear it.

JULIAN

How do you know what I'm going to say?

MICHELLE

I'm afraid of what you're going to say. I can't allow myself
to hear it.
(*pause*)
I made Charles a promise. That's what I came to tell you.
I'm going to Rome for two months. It's the least I can do
for him.

*Julian stands and looks away. Two hummingbirds flit above the ole-
ander bushes.*

Will you wait for me?

JULIAN

When are you leaving?

MICHELLE

Next Monday.

JULIAN

Will we see each other before you leave?

MICHELLE

I don't think we should.
(*beat*)
Will you wait?

*She stands and walks over to him. Two Japanese students, arm in
arm, walk past. He looks away.*

JULIAN

All my life, Michelle, I've been waiting, standing at the
ocean waiting . . .

> MICHELLE

Julian, please stop . . .

> JULIAN

. . . waiting for something on the horizon.
> (*turns to her*)

I'm a good liar, but I'm not lying now.

> MICHELLE

I'll wait for you. Tell me you'll wait for me.

> JULIAN
> (*sad and resigned*)

I don't know if I'll have a chance.

> MICHELLE

You mean because of the Palm Springs murder case. If I do
this for Charles, he won't hurt you. He may even help you.

*Julian shrugs his shoulders hopelessly. With friends like Stratton and
Leon, he needs no enemies.*

*He takes Michelle's hand and leads her over a narrow wood bridge
toward the exit.*

She pulls him to her.

> I wanted to talk about the other day. I didn't mean what I
> said. When I said I didn't want to fuck you.
> (*kisses him*)
> I want to fuck you. I wanted to fuck you then. I always
> want to fuck you.
> (*between kisses*)
> I want to fuck you now.

*Julian wraps his arms around her. They exchange a long kiss. Time
almost stops.*

CUT TO:

INT. SUNDAY'S OFFICE — DAY

A police officer escorts Julian and his lawyer into Sunday's office.

Lieutenant Curtis, a young man in a plaid suit, stands waiting in the corner. Sunday looks up from his desk.

> SUNDAY
>
> This is Lieutenant Curtis from Palm Springs. He's in charge of this case.

> JULIAN
>
> I thought you were.

> SUNDAY
>
> Not me. I'm just in charge of pimps, prostitutes, and hustlers. They keep me pretty low on the pole.

There's an awkward pause as Julian and his lawyer sit. Lieutenant Curtis is not a talkative man.

Sunday takes a dramatic pause, then looks Julian in the eye.

> You've been identified, Julian.

Julian loses his color. His casual demeanor evaporates. His lawyer reaches his arm over as if to hush him.

> JULIAN'S LAWYER
>
> Julian.

> JULIAN
> (overlapping)
>
> Who? Who could possibly identify me?

> SUNDAY
>
> You parked your Mercedes, black, 450SL, about fifty feet from the Rhyman house between 9.30 and 10.00 the night of the 22nd. Then you proceeded up the block, and entered the house.
> (beat)
> Someone saw you, Julian.

Sunday and Curtis study Julian.

> JULIAN'S LAWYER
>
> I request that formal . . . .

JULIAN
(*interrupts*)

I don't understand. Who would say such a thing? I wasn't
there.

SUNDAY

Then she identified subject number 1. Then she said she
wasn't sure which one of you it was.

Julian breathes a sigh of relief.

JULIAN'S LAWYER

But there was a black Mercedes?

SUNDAY

Convertible.

JULIAN

What was the license number?

SUNDAY

She didn't see it.

JULIAN

Damn.

Julian searches for some emotion in Curtis's face: there is none.

SUNDAY

We looked through your apartment the other day.
(*to lawyer*)
We had a warrant.

JULIAN

I know.

*Sunday pulls a letter-size envelope out of his desk and shows it to
Julian. Opening the envelope, he rifles through a stack of bills.*

SUNDAY

Recognize these?

JULIAN

No.

SUNDAY

They were found under your mattress.

Julian looks at the bills: they were planted in his room.

JULIAN

So what?

SUNDAY

They were covered with Mrs Rhyman's fingerprints.

JULIAN

I suppose you found the jewels too?

SUNDAY

What jewels?

JULIAN

I read the papers too. The jewels stolen from the Rhymans.
Whoever planted the money probably planted the jewels too.

SUNDAY

There were no jewels.

JULIAN'S LAWYER
(*to Curtis*)

Didn't you ever wonder why a supposed murderer would
keep a monogrammed envelope from his alleged victim
under his mattress?

Curtis turns to Sunday for a response.

SUNDAY

We wondered about that.

JULIAN

And that this whole thing is a frame?

SUNDAY

It occurred to us.

JULIAN

Have you checked on Rhyman himself? This sounds like
something kinky he'd get into.

Curtis breaks his silence.

> CURTIS
>
> He has an alibi. Three Palm Springs businessmen can account for his whereabouts.

> JULIAN
>
> Big deal. How about . . .?

> SUNDAY
> (*interrupts*)
>
> You're grabbing at straws, Julian.

> JULIAN
>
> How about Leon Jaimes, the spade that sent me out there?

> SUNDAY
>
> He spoke highly of you. He said you were a high-class act, not the kind to do anything dumb like this.

> JULIAN
>
> What do you think?

> SUNDAY
> (*tough*)
>
> I think you were in Palm Springs the night of the 22nd. I think you're guilty as sin. I think you went to the Rhymans, did a trick, played some rough games, got stupid or drugged or both, beat her up, killed her, stole the money and jewels.

Julian's lawyer stands.

> JULIAN'S LAWYER
>
> Then there's nothing more to talk about until you press charges.

> SUNDAY
>
> Even though we think Julian's guilty, we're not going to arrest him.

Curtis speaks.

> CURTIS
>
> For three reasons. One, we don't have enough evidence.

Two, you're easy to find. Three, if you're being framed, you're going to be a lot more use to us on the street.

Julian's lawyer stands.

JULIAN'S LAWYER
Can we go now?

Sunday turns to Curtis; Curtis nods. They start to leave.

CUT TO:

EXT. WESTWOOD APARTMENT HOTEL — DAY

Julian's Mercedes turns into the hotel drive and heads toward the parking area.

CUT TO:

INT. PARKING STRUCTURE — DAY

Julian pulls into his parking spot and gets out.

He senses someone watching him; he slowly turns, scanning the parking area.

A blond boy watches him from across the parking structure. Standing next to a dark brown Porsche, the boy wears tennis shoes, jeans, and a white T-shirt.

The blond boy looks vaguely familiar: Julian tries to remember if he's seen him before. Was he at The Probe with Leon?

The blond boy quickly gets into his Porsche and drives off.

Not bothering to lock his car, Julian heads for the hotel entrance.

CUT TO:

INT. WESTWOOD APARTMENT HOTEL LOBBY — DAY

Julian speaks to Jill at the desk.

JULIAN
The blond boy that was here last week looking for me, remember?

She thinks.

Was he about this tall?

Julian gestures. Jill remembers, then nods.

Tight little body? Kind of faggy-looking?

> JILL
> *(nods)*

Yeah.

CUT TO:

INT. WESTWOOD APARTMENT HOTEL CORRIDOR — DAY

Julian strides down the corridor, unlocks his door, and enters.

CUT TO:

INT. JULIAN'S ROOM — DAY

Julian suspiciously surveys his suite. Is anything unusual? Is anything out of place?

He walks over to the bed and yanks off the covers with one sweeping motion. Finding nothing, he lifts the king-sized mattress off the frame and heaves it against the wall.

There's nothing there.

He studies the room again. The blond boy has planted something in his room: where is it?

He methodically destroys his sanctuary. He scatters magazines, newspapers, cassettes, and cups off a coffee table and bureau.

He rips the books from his shelves.

He opens the back of his television and searches its interior. Nothing.

He rummages through his toiletries.

He opens the back of the toilet, examines the plumbing under the sink. Nothing is out of order.

Julian walks back into the bedroom and looks around. The room is a mess.

CUT TO:

INT. PARKING STRUCTURE — DAY

Julian steps back into the parking structure. Another car sits where the blond boy's Porsche was parked.

Julian steps over to the Mercedes and reaches for the handle. He senses something wrong,

Stepping back, he notices grease on his pants. And on the side of the car. Grease that wasn't there before.

Julian opens the door and examines the leather interior. He unlocks the hood, gets out, and looks at the engine. All seems in order.

He opens the trunk. Thinks. Then pulls out the mat, spare tire, and tool kit.

Inside the car, he empties the contents of the glove compartment, console, and door pockets and spreads them across the concrete. He yanks out the floor mats, rips back the carpeting. He pulls out the seat cushions.

He lies under his Mercedes with a flashlight, examining its underside. His white shirt is dirty and spotted with grease.

Auto parts are spread around the vehicle.

He pulls an oil-spotted plastic bag from the undercarriage.

Squirming from underneath the car, he opens the bag and examines its contents: two diamond bracelets, a pearl-string necklace, and several rings.

CUT TO:

EXT. HERTZ OFFICE — EVENING

Julian stands at the counter in the Hertz office at Wilshire and Westwood.

He wears work clothes.

CUT TO:

EXT. HERTZ PARKING LOT — EVENING

Julian drives his yellow Pinto up to the sidewalk and waits for the traffic to break.

He looks at himself in the rear-view mirror: his hair is too neat. He musses it up with his hand.

He pulls out of the lot and turns on Westwood Boulevard.

CUT TO:

EXT. HOLLYWOOD — NIGHT

Julian's yellow Pinto prowls the back streets of Hollywood's tenderloin: Las Palmas, Selma, Cherokee.

Young boys wait invitingly on every corner: studs in leather and choke chains, chicken-boned children, strutting little street punks. Their bodies, shrouded in neon halos, reflect off Julian's windshield. He scans the sidewalks. Boyish faces look back at him from the shadows.

He pulls alongside a hustler on Santa Monica Boulevard and asks him:

> JULIAN
> Do you know a blond kid, about this tall? Hangs out with Leon Jaimes?

The hustler shrugs. Julian drives on.

CUT TO:

EXT. LAX — NIGHT

A SAS 747 lands.

CUT TO:

EXT. BEVERLY HILLS — DAY

The next day. Julian's Pinto is parked on Camden.

He slouches in the driver's seat, watching a brown glass office building across the street.

His eyes are dark, he is unshaven. He starts to doze off, but catches himself.

Later. He gets out and walks over to a phone booth.

He drops a dime into the pay-phone, dials, and waits for the line to ring. His eyes stay fixed on the office building.

> JULIAN
> (*on phone*)
>
> Hello, Anne?
>
> > (*beat*)
>
> Yes, this is Julian.
>
> > (*beat*)
>
> Yes, yes, I know. I'm sorry.
>
> > (*beat*)
>
> I know I promised, but I just couldn't –
>
> > (*beat*)
>
> Can we get together? I need your help.
>
> > (*beat*)
>
> Perino's at 9.30?

Julian's eyes catch something across the street.

A limousine pulls in front of the office building and waits.

A moment later, Leon, wearing an unstructured suit, pushes the door open for Glenn Rhyman and they step out. Both are impeccably dressed.

> I promise I'll be there. Don't worry. Thanks again, Anne.

Rhyman gets into Leon's brown Cadillac Seville and they drive off. Julian gets into his yellow Pinto and follows.

CUT TO:

INT. WESTWOOD APARTMENT HOTEL LOBBY — DAY

Michelle stands at the desk with Jill.

> JILL
>
> I don't know where he is. Messages have been coming in
> all day. I haven't seen him since yesterday.

> MICHELLE
>
> Tell me, Jill. Please.

> JILL
>
> I don't know. Honest. I'd tell you, Michelle. The police
> were here all morning. His room's a mess.
> (*confidential*)
> There's a cop waiting outside. And another in the room.
> Julian's gonna get thrown out this time for sure.

> MICHELLE
>
> Does he call in?

> JILL
>
> Yes. But I'm not supposed to tell.

> MICHELLE
>
> When he calls in, tell him I'm looking for him. It's impor-
> tant. Ask him if there's some place we can meet.

> JILL
>
> Is there a number where he can reach you?

> MICHELLE
>
> Yes.

She writes down the number.

CUT TO:

INT. DOWNTOWN LA — DAY

*Julian's yellow Pinto follows Leon's Cadillac east on Wilshire. The
glass and steel skyscrapers of downtown Los Angeles loom in the
smoggy distance.*

Entering the downtown area, they work their way through the congested cross streets.

The Cadillac pulls up in front of the Manufacturers' Bank building on Ninth Street. The valet opens the door for Rhyman as they get out. Leon and Rhyman enter the bank building.

Julian pulls to the curb and waits.

The valet wheels the Cadillac around and drives into the underground parking structure.

Julian pulls his Pinto into a nearby parking lot.

    CUT TO:

EXT. DOWNTOWN PARKING LOT — DAY

A parking attendant directs Julian to a spot.

He parks and gets out. He pulls a pair of work gloves from his back pocket and puts them on. He opens the car door, reaches inside, and pulls out the oil-spotted bag of Rhyman jewels.

He tucks the jewels into his pocket and walks across the street toward the bank.

He enters the underground parking structure.

    CUT TO:

INT. UNDERGROUND PARKING STRUCTURE — DAY

Julian slips past the parking attendants and heads toward the VIP parking section.

Crouching down, he edges his way along a row of Rolls Royces, Mercedes, and black limos.

He spots Rhyman's car, looks around quickly, and crawls underneath. He pulls out the bag of jewels and plants them under the car.

His job completed, Julian pulls himself from under the Cadillac and tucks his gloves into his back pocket.

Across the parking structure, another attendant steps out of the mens' room and walks toward the VIP parking section.

Julian stands up, sees the attendant, and works his way through the cars in the opposite direction.

The parking attendant calls to him:

> PARKING ATTENDANT

Hey!

Julian pretends not to hear him.

What are you doing there?

The attendant catches up with him.

I asked you a question, boy.

Julian affects a Latin-American accent and a menial's slouch.

> JULIAN

I like to watch the big cars.

The attendant thinks a moment, then dismisses him.

> PARKING ATTENDANT

OK. Beat it.

Julian walks out of the parking structure.

> CUT TO:

EXT. PERINO'S — NIGHT

The valet opens the door as a young lady dressed in Alaskan fur steps out of a Jaguar.

Julian, having parked his Pinto down the block, walks past the valet and enters.

> CUT TO:

INT. PERINO'S — NIGHT

Julian brushes his hair into place as he steps into the exclusive restaurant. His work clothes are soiled; he has two days' growth on his face.

The maître d' *looks at him in surprise.*

MAÎTRE D'

Julian?

Julian fishes in his pocket, pulls out a ten, and slips it into the maître d's *palm.*

JULIAN

Yeah. I was working and forgot about time. Got a reservation for me?

The maître d', *still puzzled by Julian's appearance, leads him to a booth where Anne waits.*

Julian plops down next to Anne and sighs.

ANNE

Julie, you look like shit. What's wrong?

JULIAN

Everything.
                    (*to waiter*)
I'll have a straight bourbon.

ANNE

What are you doing to yourself? The way you look now, you couldn't get a maid to fuck you.

JULIAN

I need your help, Anne. The cops are after me. They've got me framed for the Rhyman murder.

ANNE

Where were you yesterday?

JULIAN

What do you mean?

ANNE

Mrs Vaffklar. She came in yesterday afternoon on a SAS

flight from Stockholm, and there was no one at the airport to meet her. She was furious. The Saab people are
furious. I've got hell to pay. What happened? Didn't you
prepare?

*Julian can hardly believe what he's hearing. He's at the end of his
tether, and she's talking about some trick he missed.*

JULIAN

Didn't you hear me, Anne? The cops are after me. I'm on
borrowed time.

ANNE

So you stand me up? Without even bothering to call?

The waiter brings Julian's drink.

JULIAN
(*exasperated*)

Jesus Christ.

He looks around the room. He sees the face he is looking for.

*Michelle sits alone in a distant booth. She looks desperately at
Julian, mouthing the words, 'I must talk to you.'*

ANNE
(*looking at menu*)

What do you want?

JULIAN
(*nods to Michelle*)

Just the chopped salad. Are you going to help me?

ANNE

I've checked around, Julie. You are in trouble.

JULIAN

That's why I need your help.

ANNE

You never did anything for me.

JULIAN
(*incredulous*)
Never did anything for you? I'm your number-one boy.

ANNE
You fight me every turn. Screw me whenever you can. You ask a favor, then stand up a gig I worked for six months to set up.

JULIAN
(*watching Michelle*)
I explained that.

ANNE
I'm through with you, Julie. You'll have to fend for your-self. I don't care what happens to you any more.

Michelle stands and walks past Julian and Anne's booth on her way to the restrooms. She nods for Julian to follow.

JULIAN
How can you replace me?

ANNE
It won't be hard. You like to think your clients are discrim-inating, but they really aren't. Any boy will do.

Julian's eyes follow Michelle as Anne speaks.

JULIAN
(*stands*)
Excuse me a second.

He follows Michelle's path. He walks up the carpeted steps and turns at the top of the stairs.

He hesitates a moment, then pushes the door reading 'Ladies' and enters.

CUT TO:

INT. PERINO'S RESTROOM — NIGHT

Julian quickly surveys the powder room: fortunately, it's empty.

Except for Michelle. She waits across the room.

> MICHELLE

Julian.

He picks up the wood doorstop and wedges it into the door jamb. She embraces him.

> Thank God you got my message. I've been looking for you all day.

> JULIAN
> (*holding her*)

It's all right, baby.

> MICHELLE
> (*distraught*)

No, no, it's not. John talked to the DA. They've found the murder weapon. They're going to arrest you.

A flash of pain crosses Julian's face.

> JULIAN

That can't be.

> MICHELLE

What are you going to do?

> JULIAN

I don't know.

A woman tries to enter the ladies' room. Julian puts his hand on the door wedge. The door budges but doesn't open. The woman walks away.

> MICHELLE

How can I help you?

> JULIAN

There's nothing you can do . . .

> MICHELLE

There must be something . . .

Julian interrupts her curtly. If he's going under, there's no reason to take her along. Desperation can give rise to rare acts of altruism. So can love.

> JULIAN
> (*takes her by the shoulders*)
> You don't understand. I'm in deep trouble. Stay away from me.

> MICHELLE
> (*protesting*)
> No . . .

> JULIAN
> There's going to be a *scandal*. Don't have anything to do with me. I'll ruin your life. And your husband's. It's all over.

> MICHELLE
> Not if you're innocent.

He takes her face in his hands.

> JULIAN
> Look at me, baby. How do you know I'm innocent? How can you be so sure?

> MICHELLE
> But you are innocent . . .

He holds her face in a vice-like grip.

> JULIAN
> Look at my face. Can you tell me without any hesitation whatsoever that you know I'm innocent?

> MICHELLE
> Yes.

Julian is overwhelmed: he has never been this loved.

> JULIAN
> Forget me. Stay away from me.
> (*his eyes are moist*)
> I never loved you.

He uses this opportunity to turn away from her and pull the wedge out of the door jamb. He must leave now before they both break down.

A woman pushes the door open, stumbles into the restroom. She looks up at Julian in surprise.

He walks out. Michelle, stunned, watches him.

CUT TO:

INT. PERINO'S — NIGHT

Julian storms past a waiter and walks out of the restaurant. His face is blitzed with emotions. He tries to hold them back.

Anne and the maître d' *watch him as he goes.*

CUT TO:

EXT. LEON'S APARTMENT — DAWN

Julian's yellow Pinto is parked on the Wilshire high-rise row east of Westwood village.

Julian, half-asleep, watches Leon's apartment building. He looks like a zombie. He's been up all night.

About dawn, Leon's Cadillac turns into his apartment's parking structure. Julian slouches further in the front seat.

Ten seconds later, another car pulls into Leon's apartment: a dark brown Porsche driven by the blond boy. Julian watches intently.

He gets out of the Pinto and walks toward the apartment high-rise.

CUT TO:

INT. LEON'S APARTMENT

There's a knock on the door. Leon, wearing an unstructured yellow suit, a bright blue shirt, and red snakeskin boots, opens the door a crack.

Julian's unshaven face appears through the crack.

                              LEON
                           (*surprised*)
Julian.

                             JULIAN
Let me in, Leon. It's important.

Leon unchains the door.

                              LEON
Julie, you look terrible. You want to clean up? Get a shave?

*Julian steps into the chrome-and-glass Contempo apartment. An
Andy Warhol lithograph of Martin Luther King hangs over the fireplace.*

*The blond boy, standing beside the Warhol print, sees Julian enter
and walks into the bedroom. Julian catches him out of the corner of
his eye.*

                             JULIAN
I hate to bug you this time of morning, Leon, but this is
important.

                              LEON
I'm listening.

                             JULIAN
You got my alibi ready? I'm going to need it today.

                              LEON
                           (*hedging*)
It's not ready yet, Julie. Tomorrow. I'm piecing it together.
It's not easy, you know . . .

                             JULIAN
                          (*interrupting*)
Why are you trying to frame me?

                              LEON
What are you talking about?

                             JULIAN
Judy Rhyman's murder. You're behind it.

LEON

You're crazy.

JULIAN

You and Rhyman.

Leon starts to protest.

And that blond little boyfriend of yours. The one that was
just here. The one in the brown Porsche who planted the
money and jewels . . .

LEON

I don't know what you're talking about.

JULIAN

He's the one that actually killed her, isn't he? Got into a
scene with Rhyman and his wife. Got a little rough and
killed her. Then you had to get somebody to take the fall.
Couldn't be the boy, couldn't be Rhyman, so . . .

LEON
(*angry*)

Don't give me this shit. I've been worked over three times
by the cops on this case. I'm clean.

JULIAN

I don't care who killed Judy Rhyman. Just answer me
one question: how much do I have to pay to get off the
hook?

LEON

You ain't talking about money, you're talking about murder. You killed a bitch and now you're gonna pay the consequences.

JULIAN

How much?

LEON

I'm sorry for you, Julian.

                              JULIAN
                             (*urgent*)
How much?

Leon looks at Julian coldly. His hatred hovers just beneath the surface of his chiseled black face.

                              LEON
     It don't matter how much, Julie. The other side will
     always pay me more.

Leon smiles. He's supremely arrogant. The frame is perfect: there's nothing Julian can do about it.

                              JULIAN
     You got the frame on pretty tight, don't you, Leon?

Leon nods.

     You're pretty proud of yourself, aren't you? You've done a
     good job.

                              LEON
     Just helping the police catch a murderer. The parking
     attendant saw you planting the jewels on his car, Julie.
     The police found the murder weapon – a gold statue – in
     the trash behind your hotel.
                             (*beat*)
     And that broad in Palm Springs is going to change her
     mind any time now – and identify you.

                              JULIAN
                             (*pleading*)
     What do you want, Leon? This is my life! You know what
     they'll do to me in jail, don't you?

Leon smiles.

                              LEON
                             (*cruel*)
I know.

JULIAN

I'm worth twenty–thirty grand. It's all yours.

Leon has no comment.

I met a Spanish kid the other day. A beautiful boy. Seven-teen-year-old. I already broke him in. He did a trick with Mrs Jarvie. He's all yours.
> (*no comment*)

I'll break in new boys for you. I'll work just for you on a forty–sixty split.
> (*no comment*)

Thirty–seventy. I'll do fag tricks. I'll do kink tricks. I'll do whatever you want me to do.

Leon walks out on the sun deck, then looks back at Julian.

LEON

Leave me alone, Julian. Get out.

JULIAN

Your blond trick killed her, didn't he? He and Rhyman together.

LEON

It doesn't matter now.

JULIAN
(*following him*)
Why was it me, Leon? Why did you pick me to frame?

Leon looks across the misty Los Angeles horizon. The sun will soon be rising. He turns back to Julian.

LEON

Because you were frameable, Julie. You'd stepped on too many toes. Nobody cared about you.
> (*beat*)

I never liked you much myself. Now get out.

Leon's eye catches something on the narrow strip of lawn twelve floors down. He makes a subtle gesture to the person down below – which Julian notices.

JULIAN
Who's out there? Your new boy?

Julian charges toward Leon.

Tell me, you motherfucker!

Julian hits Leon full force just as he is leaning over the railing.

Leon's arms flail about. One hits Julian square in the face. Leon starts to sink over the far side. His wallet and change slip from his coat, falling to the pavement twelve stories below.

LEON
Help! Help!

Julian, sinking to his knees, grabs Leon's waist through the iron bars.

The black man's 200-pound frame sinks through Julian's hands. Julian clings to Leon's knees.

Save me! I'll do anything!

Julian desperately struggles to pull Leon up. Looking down, he sees the blond boy standing twelve floors below, watching them. Day is breaking.

Leon sinks lower. Julian clasps him around the calves. Leon's arms wave meaninglessly about.

Help!

Grimacing, Julian maniacally tries to pull Leon back. Leon is his only proof of innocence.

The huge black man sinks lower. Julian's arms are just above his high-heeled red snakeskin boots.

Leon gives out a strangled yelp as his body pops out of his boots and plunges headlong toward Wilshire Boulevard.

A moment is suspended in time as Leon's yellow form slowly drifts downward. Then – splat – it hits the pavement almost anticlimactically.

Julian, pulling himself up, drops one of the red boots. It falls to the pavement, bouncing several feet away from Leon's body.

Julian, holding the second boot, stands against the railing.

He hears the screech of tires and looks down.

The dark brown Porsche wheels around Leon's body and speeds down Wilshire. In a moment it is gone.

Julian walks slowly back into the apartment.

He sits on the large white sofa, cradling Leon's red snakeskin boot between his legs.

Outside, cars screech to a halt. Soon there are the sounds of police sirens.

Later. Footsteps are heard in the hall. Police enter the room and fan out. One rushes to the railing.

An officer walks over to Julian. He looks up hopelessly.

JULIAN
I want to talk to Detective Sunday, Homicide.

CUT TO:

EXT. WEST LA POLICE DEPARTMENT — DAY

Purdue Street is a mass of chaos. Still photographers fight with radio reporters and TV cameramen for a glimpse of Los Angeles' newest media celebrity: Julian Kay, American gigolo, servicer of the rich, accused murderer.

Julian, dressed in prison clothes, is pushed from a police van. His hands are handcuffed and chained to his waist.

He is pulled by two burly plain clothes men through the mob of reporters and cameramen. They shout questions at him.

REPORTER #1
Is it true you serviced 400 women?

REPORTER #2
How much did you charge, Julian?

REPORTER #3
How many clients do you have?

REPORTER #4
Are you innocent?

REPORTER #5
Did you work for movie stars?

REPORTER #1
How many women did you service in a week?

Julian shields his eyes and looks down as if in shame. The plain clothes men haul him into the police station.

CUT TO:

INT. SUNDAY'S OFFICE

Julian sits next to his lawyer in the interrogation room. Sunday and Lieutenant Curtis sit across the table. Spread across the table are:

– the oil-spotted plastic bag of jewels;

– the gold statuette from Judy Rhyman's bedstand, now registered as the murder weapon;

– copies of the Los Angeles Times *and the* Herald Examiner. *One bold headline screams:* 'GIGOLO CHARGED IN PALM SPRINGS SEX SLAYING.' *A follow-up story promises:* 'JULIAN KAY'S CLIENTS: THE RICH AND THE POWERFUL.'

SUNDAY
I wish I had arrested you earlier. It would have been easier on you.

JULIAN'S LAWYER
You better help the judge put an end to this pre-trial publicity or we'll never have a fair trial.

CURTIS
We're moving him to Palm Springs today.

SUNDAY
(*to Julian*)
Do you have anything to say, Julian?

Julian has lost the desire to fight back. He is resigned. He has accepted his fate. He shakes his head.

JULIAN
(*half-hearted*)
No.

The film begins a series of fade out/fade ins.

FADE OUT.

FADE IN:

INT. PRISON VISITORS' ROOM

Michelle and Julian look at each other through the wire mesh. At first there is only silence.

JULIAN
Are you going on your trip?

MICHELLE
No. I decided not to.

Pause.

JULIAN
Does your husband know you're here?

MICHELLE
No.

JULIAN
Why did you come?

MICHELLE
(*pause*)
I have nowhere else to go. I'm all alone.

There is another pause. Julian looks at her as if she were a foreign land.

I didn't think I'd ever see you again.

> JULIAN
> (*without emotion*)
> Don't come back, Michelle.

She fights back tears.

> MICHELLE
> (*pause*)
> Are you satisfied with your lawyer?

> JULIAN
> It doesn't matter.

A prison guard walks into the visitors' room and approaches Julian. Michelle starts to rise; Julian's stoic resolve starts to weaken. His eyes reach toward her. He says tenderly, almost desperately:

> Don't go.

The guard taps Julian on the shoulder and he realizes he must leave. He stands and walks off with the guard.

FADE OUT.

FADE IN:

INT. PRISON VISITORS' ROOM — DAY

Julian's lawyer and Michelle's lawyer, an older, well-dressed veteran of many criminal cases, sit outside the wire mesh.

> MICHELLE'S LAWYER
> Michelle Stratton is paying for my services, Julian. I think you know this is a matter of some secrecy.

> JULIAN
> (*without emotion*)
> Tell her not to bother.

JULIAN'S LAWYER

Julian, you'll have to help us more.

JULIAN

Tell Michelle to forget me.

MICHELLE'S LAWYER

Frankly, Julian, I'm more worried about your defense than I am about Mrs Stratton's private life. We have to go through the details of the night of the murder – your every movement.

JULIAN'S LAWYER

If you really want to help Julian, you'll get some of this heat off.

MICHELLE'S LAWYER

What do you mean?

JULIAN'S LAWYER

The newspapers and TV are trying him in the media. If they'll ease off a bit, perhaps we can put some of the pieces together: Leon, Rhyman, the blond boy – he's the key.

They turn back to Julian: he says nothing.

FADE OUT.

FADE IN:

INT. LIEUTENANT CURTIS'S OFFICE – DAY

A Palm Springs policeman leads Michelle into Lieutenant Curtis's office.

MICHELLE

Lieutenant Curtis?

CURTIS

Yes, Mrs Stratton. This is an honor. I was told you wanted to see me. What can I do for you?

> MICHELLE

I want to talk to you about the Julian Kay/Rhyman murder case.

> CURTIS

Yes?

> MICHELLE

I'm paying for Mr Kay's legal defense.

> CURTIS
> (*knowingly*)

Um-hm.

> MICHELLE

I'm paying for Mr Kay's defense because I know he is not
guilty. I do not wish to see an obstruction of justice.

> CURTIS

How do you know he's not guilty?

> MICHELLE

Because he was not in Palm Springs the 22nd, the night of
the murder.

> CURTIS

No?

> MICHELLE

No. He was with me.

FADE OUT.

FADE IN:

INT. PRISON VISITORS' ROOM — DAY

Curtis leads Michelle over to Julian. He waits behind the wire mesh.

> MICHELLE

I told them, Julian.

> JULIAN

I heard.

> (*beat*)
Tu n'avais pas besoin de faire ça, Michelle. Tu peux le dementir.

MICHELLE

Jamais. Plutôt mourir.

Pause.

JULIAN

What will you do now?

MICHELLE

I don't know. I can't go home.
> (*beat*)
The newsmen are waiting outside for me. There's dozens of them.

Julian's voice cracks.

JULIAN

Why did you do it?

MICHELLE

I had no choice.
> (*draws close to him*)
I love you.

She places her fingers in the wire mesh.

Julian passionately kisses the knuckles on one hand, then the other. He kisses her forehead.

All this time, Julian has prepared himself for the explosion – but it never came. Instead, far more powerful, comes the implosion.

His hands tremble as they touch hers. His eyes are moist.

JULIAN
> (*kissing her forehead*)
Oh, Michelle, it's taken me so long to come to you.

FADE OUT.

Light Sleeper

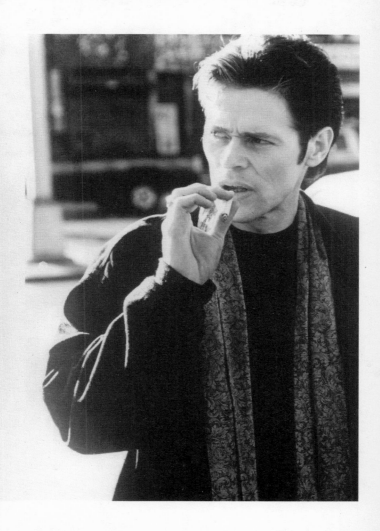

CAST AND CREW

MAIN CAST

LETOUR	Willem Dafoe
ANN	Susan Sarandon
MARIANNE	Dana Delany
ROBERT	David Clennon
TERESA	Mary Beth Hurt
TIS	Victor Garber
RANDI	Jane Adams

MAIN CREW

Written and Directed by	Paul Schrader
Produced by	Linda Reisman
Executive Producer	Mario Kassar
Co-Executive Producer	Ronna B. Wallace
Co-Producer	G. Mac Brown
Edited by	Kristina Boden
Director of Photography	Ed Lachman
Production Designer	Richard Hornung
Music by	Michael Been
Casting by	Ellen Chenoweth

'Behold I show you a mystery; we shall not all sleep, but we shall all be changed.'

I. Corinthians 15:51

John LeTour, forty, light sleeper. Never meant to be a drug dealer; it just came along. He's been other things: messenger boy, cab driver, model, postal clerk, doorman, nightclub shill – never meant to be them either. Now he's a D.D. Drug dealer.

John LeTour, well-groomed, khaki slacks, leather jacket, tippet-like scarf, belt pouch, 'Beatle' boots, a shadow drifting in and out of other shadows, New York, day, night: watching, listening, rarely speaking – non-existent, seen only by those he sees. His face an affable blank. Make of it what you will. The eyes flicker; the hands shift discreetly. A map of calculation. Once he had a drug problem. Life turned a page. Today he follows instructions: he sleeps light – one eye open, anticipating.

John LeTour, D.D., loner, voyeur, has been drifting toward an unknown destination. At mid-life the destination draws near. The circle tightens. The dealer is anxious. The destination is love.

A NIGHT IN THE LIFE

Credit sequence: New York by night. John LeTour nestles in back of a blue car-service sedan, face reflected in the window. Neon mixes with steam, street people with tourists, young dates: each with a different agenda, a hidden purpose. His beeper goes off. He clicks it, checks the digital message.

The driver stops at an uptown corner. LeTour opens the curbside door, motions to the driver he'll be back in 'ten' minutes. He enters the video laundromat, a twenty-four-hour video rental/laundromat/ tanning salon.

Inside, he meets a retro-yuppie (J. Crew Division) in the 'Classics' section. They exit.

On the sidewalk, money is exchanged for a packet. LeTour pockets the uncounted cash. The yuppie mouths goodbye, eager to put dis-

tance between him and LeTour. John checks his beeper, stops at a pay-phone, dials.

John LeTour re-enters the sedan; the driver heads downtown. High-rises give way to Tudor City. Uncollected trash lines the curbs. LeTour eyes a pedestrian; pedestrian looks back.

Later. 3 a.m. The streets are dark. LeTour's car passes a glowing Korean market.

LeTour narrates from diary:

> LETOUR (V.O.)
> Labor Day weekend. Some time for a sanitation strike. Everybody crazy to stock up. They decide to score at the last minute and want it now. Never fails. The faces look alike. You gotta use memory tricks: each has some peculiarity – it keeps you sharp. A D.D. told me when a drug dealer starts writing a diary it's time to quit. I started writing after that. Not every night – now and then. Just to burn off the night. Fill up one book, throw it out, start another.

The sedan drives on. End credits.

CUT TO:

HOMEBASE

4 a. m.: streets empty. Le Tour's sedan drops him off near a ten-story West 80s apartment building. John gives the driver a forty-dollar tip (standard procedure), turns the corner. He presses the intercom; a buzzer unlocks the door. He enters the lobby, walks past English reproduction furniture toward the elevators. Presses the button.

Penthouse C door opens. Ann lets John in with a smile. Ann, forty-four, striking in a tailored dress, greets him with a wet kiss. Her hair is coiffured, her face made up. She is John's employer, mentor, confidante, Mother Hen: she keeps the books. Her ingenuous demeanor belies sterner stuff: she's been in the drug business fifteen years.

Ann's apartment is a jumble of sensibilities: dark green walls, zebra-

skin sofa, Haitian wall friezes, framed magazine photos of Parama-
hansa Yogananda, Liz Taylor, the Duke of Windsor – paintings
stacked behind an oversized urn. A bird flits in its cage. One corner
of the living area is devoted to a fledgling cosmetics business: Macin-
tosh computer, billboard of trade paper clippings and ads, herbal
samples, reference books, color charts.

Robert, fifty, slight, waves hello as John locks the door. Gay, hip,
worn, he's John's 'co-runner.'

They work – and eat – out of Ann's apartment. Take-out tins of
Indian food are stacked amid crystals, tarot cards, glasses, and vita-
min bottles. No sign of drugs, drug paraphernalia, or money.

ANN

Darling.

LETOUR

Ann.

ANN

Have we made New York safe for another weekend?

LETOUR
(waves)

Robert.

ROBERT

Get a job.

LETOUR
(about Robert)

Sad what ten years without sex can do.

Repartee: the plumbing of family feeling.

John unzips his belt pouch, walks toward the bedroom to deposit the
night's earnings.

ANN

Any hundreds?

LETOUR

Twenties – and tens.

                              ROBERT
Tens!

                              ANN
Goddamn cash machines.

                              ROBERT
Did what's-his-name give you a hard time?

                         LETOUR (O.S.)
You mean –?

                              ROBERT
Yeah.

                              LETOUR
Cash Before Delivery.
                         (*re-emerges*)
CBD.

                              ROBERT
Fucking investment bankers.

                              ANN
These Wall Street kids deal with fake money all day, they
think cash is a theoretical concept – like it doesn't apply. I
see 'em at two, shudder to think at nine they're buying
and selling – turned me off the stock market.

                              LETOUR
It's late.
                         (*to Robert*)
You staying?

                              ROBERT
It's over.

                              LETOUR
I'm gonna crash – try, at least.

                              ANN
                         (*to LeTour*)
Tomorrow will be easier. Maybe we can all eat together.

Go on. You look tired. Here, take a couple of Cs. I'll pick
up anything that comes in.

LeTour turns to leave.

Sleep tight.

ROBERT

Pick up the trash.

LETOUR
(laughs)

Yeah – big kiss.

He throws two kisses, exits.

CUT TO:

JOHN'S APARTMENT

*First light reflects across the Hudson as LeTour walks west on 22nd
Street toward his Chelsea apartment building. A delivery truck
passes uncollected garbage. He enters a nondescript doorway. Inside
his studio apartment, John sits at a second-hand table writing in a
composition book. He drinks from an eight-ounce glass of white
wine, continues.*

*The room has little personality; Ann's apartment has enough for
two. Nails indicate where pictures once hung; a boom box sits on the
linoleum floor amid cassettes, books* (Autobiography of a Yogi,
The Secret Doctrine), *fashion magazines, a stack of unopened
CDs. A futon is unrolled beneath the room's sole decoration, a poster
of a human foot advertising a forgotten photo exhibit. Wine bottles –
Chenin Blanc. Precious little to show for forty years.*

Le Tour's narration resumes as he writes.

LETOUR (V.O.)

'Labor Day.' 'Union Movement' – there's a contradiction
in terms. I know about long hours. It's worse when I'm off
– I just walk and walk. Where am I going? There's an ele-
ment of providence to it all. Like rolling numbers. Luck.
You're walking down the street, some guy that looks

maybe a little like you does a stick-up four hours ago, there's an APB description out and a cop pulls you in 'cause he's cold and wants to go inside – they grab your stash. Your number's up. You're busted for nothing. For bad luck.

CUT TO:

JEALOUS

5 p.m. A Clinton transient hotel.

Inside hotel room, Le Tour meets with Jealous, a twenty-five-year-old drug intermediary in leather jacket. John counts hundred-dollar bills, hands them to Jealous.

> JEALOUS
>
> Are they 'faced'?

> LETOUR
>
> Don't bore me.

Jealous rearranges the hundreds.

> JEALOUS
>
> Is it so much work to face them the same direction? You don't do it, I got to. It's time – my time –

> LETOUR
> (*overlap*)
>
> Jees –

> JEALOUS
>
> We've been through all this.

Le Tour shrugs.

> This nineteen-gram shit is a drag.

> LETOUR
>
> We pay you more, you put up with more. White drugs for white people. Twice the price, twice the safety.

JEALOUS

I can't believe Ann's been working as long as she has –
never busted. She's something.

LETOUR

Never made any big money either.

JEALOUS

Sure.

LETOUR

She blows it.

JEALOUS

You believe that? What you gonna do after she quits? How
long you been with her?

LETOUR

She always says that. We'll see, Jealous.

JEALOUS

She's out. You should pick up her trade. You're too old to
be a go-fer. They know you, they trust you.

LETOUR

No way. I'm not the management type. I get in charge, I'll
start using again – not for me. I know music people. I'm
gonna get in recording.

JEALOUS

Yeah.

LeTour reaches for the door.

Tour.

LETOUR

What?

JEALOUS

Normally this wouldn't matter to you, but you may get
hassled.

LETOUR

Why?

JEALOUS

You read the papers? The Park murder. All over the *Post*.
Mariah Rangel – nineteen-year-old Barnard co-ed bitch
dead in Turtle Pond coked to the fucking gills. All of a
sudden they're hot after mid-level dealers. They're
buzzin'. You know her?

LETOUR
(shrugs)

I look like an encyclopedia? Who knows?
(opens door)
Thanks for the warning.

CUT TO:

THE NIGHT BEGINS

*Ann's apartment. 8 p.m. She opens the door for LeTour, kisses him,
goes back to the phone. Mantra muzak plays as John locks door,
heads toward bedroom. Inside bedroom, MTV glows silently as
Robert, wearing a black turtleneck, works at a desk amid tools of the
trade: digital scale, 'hot box,' Deering grinder, block of manite, pure
cocaine, pills, felt pen. Robert scissors glossy magazine paper* (Elle)
*into neat quarters, folds each into gram-size 'bindels' – envelopes.
Red satin drapes the ceiling.*

ROBERT

Jack.

John kisses him atop the head.

You pick up from Jealous?

LETOUR
(passes bag)

Yeah, nineteen grams after four times last night. We're certainly not his favorite people.

ROBERT

We don't make the laws. Nineteen is carrying, twenty is
dealing. Let him be stupid.

LETOUR

He took my hundreds.

ROBERT
(*stands*)

Take over for a while. I'm getting contact high.

LETOUR
(*sits*)

Who's Her Majesty talking to?

Robert flips through cable channels as John grinds cocaine.

ROBERT

The Ecstasy connection. From Arizona. She's trying to get
them to come here – or, better, Europe.

LETOUR

That's where the money is.

ROBERT

All mark-up – the 'Big One.'

LETOUR
(*laughs*)

Don't dress.
(*beat*)

You really think she means it?

ROBERT

That's what she says. New Year's Eve and out – no Acid
House, no product, no deliveries.

LETOUR

That's just her mouth talking.

ROBERT

Next year – strictly Akasha.

LETOUR

'Akasha'?

ROBERT

Cosmetics. That's what Ann's calling the company now –

LETOUR
(*interjects*)

– this week. I don't get it – marigolds, violets, sage – why'd anyone pay to put weeds on their face?

ROBERT

Why'd anyone pay to put them up their nose? I like cosmetics. I *need* cosmetics. You should come in with us.

LETOUR

You forget: she hasn't asked me.

Ann hangs up, calls:

ANN (O.S.)

Johnny! Robert! Come here!

They return to the living area.

(*open arms*)

Plant me two kisses, boys, fifteen hundred Ex at thirty each and the delivery's here.

They simultaneously kiss her cheeks.

(*to LeTour*)

Whatja think?

LETOUR

Of what?

ANN

The face cream. Almond, marigold, chamomile, egg, aloe – the 'Almilk' formula. I remixed it.

LETOUR
(*smells her*)

Very nice.

ANN

Reminds me, if you get downtown stop at Enhancements
and pick up some almond oil – not the California.
                    (*fishes menus from desk*)
What should we order?

LETOUR

How about Indian?

ANN

Darling, it's Saturday.

ROBERT

Thai. We haven't had Thai in a while.

The phone rings. Ann's voice repeats a recorded message:

ANN'S VOICE

'Hello. This is Ann. If you leave a message, we'll get back
to you – sooner than you think.'

*Answering machine beeps. Man's voice speaks from the tiny
speaker:*

ANNE'S VOICE

'Ann, this is Ed. Call me. 749-2876.'

ANN
                    (*to Robert*)
Answer that. He'll call back every five minutes.

ROBERT
                    (*walking*)
The night begins.

The phone rings again: another message as Ann examines the menu.

ANN

'Ped Srilom'? – it's Northeastern. Duck.

LETOUR
                    (*glancing*)
I'm going veggie. Get me the 'Puk Ob.'

ROBERT (O.S.)
(*from phone*)

Me too.

LETOUR

Use it for facial cream.

ROBERT (O.S.)

Remove unsightly hair!

ANN

Laugh, one day you'll be watching me on *Oprah* from a welfare hotel.

LETOUR

Forgive us.

ROBERT
(*returns*)

Eddie wants now. Now. His place. Top Lady. God knows what happened to his shit yesterday.

ANN
(*to LeTour*)

You take it – call in.

LETOUR

It was supposed to be light tonight.

ROBERT

Don't you watch TV?

LETOUR

Don't have one.

ROBERT

Well, if you were the normal stupid fuck you should be so lucky to be and had one, you'd know it's supposed to rain –

ANN

Good for the trees –

ROBERT

Some farmer whacked his numerology on us.

ANN
(*peers through curtain*)

It's started.

ROBERT

The Farmer's Almanac is based on numerology.

LETOUR

Raining?

ANN

Take a coat.
(*to Robert*)
And you, clean up the product before the food delivery
comes.

John grabs his belt pouch, heads for the closet.

CUT TO:

CONFESSOR LETOUR

*Rain falls on LeTour's car near an East Side luxury high-rise. The
door opens to Eddie's apartment: severe decor, once chic, now dated.
Eddie, thirty-two, is a mess: puffy face, sweaty shirt, pinched lips –
on a drug jag.*

EDDIE

LeTour! – finally. What took so long?

LETOUR
(*steps inside*)

Traffic. It's raining.

EDDIE

How's things?

LETOUR

OK.

EDDIE

I need a quarter – you got it?

                           LETOUR
                           (*nods*)
Robert said he sold you a quarter yesterday.

                           EDDIE
                           (*slurs*)
Some friends came over. How much is that? Fourteen
hundred?

*LeTour nods as Eddie, employing diminished skills, counts from a
roll of twenties. John looks around: full ashtrays, porn tapes, empty
vodka bottles – there have been no 'friends.'*

                           LETOUR
Eddie. Look at yourself. Sit down. I've known you, what,
like eight years?

                           EDDIE
                           (*counting*)
Yeah . . .

                           LETOUR
Knew you from the other job, the one before the last one
you fucked up. I knew your wife – remember her? We used
to sit and talk and talk –

He pressures Eddie into chair.

                           EDDIE
                           (*whining*)
You don't know what she was like –

                           LETOUR
This is no good. I'll sell you a gram and some downs, but
I ain't gonna put you in the emergency room. Cool it. Go
to bed. Sleep it off.

John's beeper goes off.

                           EDDIE
                           (*stands*)
You charge $200 for what goes for ninety on the street –
and you're not gonna sell?

> LETOUR
> (*clicks beeper*)

So go to the street.

> EDDIE

I'll call Ann.

> LETOUR

Go ahead. You know what she'll say. Phone's over there.

> EDDIE
> (*irrational*)

I'll tell the fucking cops.

> LETOUR
> (*flashes cold*)

Fuck you. That's it. You're out.
> (*turns to leave*)

Don't call again. Catch you next lifetime.

> EDDIE
> (*contrite*)

Please, Tour, I'm sorry. You're right. I didn't mean that.
I'm quitting anyway. I'll take the gram. Sorry.

> LETOUR
> (*turns back*)

OK.

> EDDIE

Two hundred?

LeTour nods.

*Eddie counts $200 as LeTour takes a gram from his pouch and gives
it to him.*

> LETOUR

You got downs?

Eddie nods.

One more thing. I gotta use the phone.

Eddie pockets the envelope as John, checking his beeper, walks to the phone.

Later. LeTour sits in an Upper West Side apartment as an earnest mid-twentyish man, wearing undershorts, snorts a hefty line, offering a rolled dollar bill as he talks. LeTour declines.

> MID-TWENTYISH MAN
> (*continuing*)

. . . but – if there's no God, how can man conceive of him? The idea of God presupposes the existence of God. That's the Ontological Argument. Anselm. Twelve hundred. Fourteen hundred – I'm not sure –

> LETOUR
> (*checks his watch*)

I've got to go.

> MID-TWENTYISH MAN
> (*gesturing*)

Let me finish. OK, if the idea of God is implanted by God – the *sensus divinitatus*, the sense of the divine – what is the role of human thought? Not faith, thought . . .

LeTour's mind drifts. His diary voice overlaps:

> LETOUR (V.O.)

Everybody wants to talk. It's like a compulsion. My philosophy is: you got nothing to say, don't say it. They figure you can tell a D.D. anything, things they would never tell anyone else. He understands. Of course they're stoned to start. If I could tie together all the hours of coke talk I've heard, that would be a lot of string. It was Robert's idea to add twenty-five dollars to home deliveries 'cause it's such a hassle. Fifty is more like it.

Later. Narration continues as sedan drives through rain.

Later. A Tribeca loft. LeTour swaps drug jargon with two NYU students at an impromptu party. Attractive ingenues drift by. Trendy twosome, blasted, sways to techno-rap.

Business done, LeTour turns to leave. The first student grabs his shoulder.

> FIRST STUDENT
>
> C'mon, Tour, stick around.

> SECOND STUDENT
>
> Yeah.

> FIRST STUDENT
>
> There's only four of us and like seven of them – and we're paying for the dope. See her, over there, the blonde, long hair, yellow skirt? – she's gonna model for Elite.

Downtown nymph, sixteen going on seventeen.

> LETOUR
> (*smiling*)
>
> Me? I'm an old man. She'd break me like an old horse.

> SECOND STUDENT
>
> Shit, dude –

> LETOUR
>
> Nah. Thanks anyway.
> (*checks watch*)
> I gotta go. Have fun.

He heads toward exit.

CUT TO:

A FACE FROM THE PAST

Le Tour's sedan heads down Lexington Avenue. It rains unabated. Puddles glisten; red tail-lights refract on the windshield. John rests in the back, a bag from Enhancements beside him.

Pedestrians, well-dressed and casual, desperately wave for taxis amid sacks of garbage. No use: nothing for blocks.

John's sedan stops for a midtown light. LeTour looks out the window, sees a woman vainly hailing a cab. He looks again. She turns her head. He recognizes her.

LETOUR
(*to driver*)

Carlos. Wait a second.

He leans over, opens the far door, calls:

Marianne! Marianne! Hop in! I'll give you a ride.

Marianne Jost, thirty-five, stylish in short black hair and long black coat, steps closer, looking through the rain.

John. John LeTour.

MARIANNE
(*recognizes him*)

John?

LETOUR

Get in. You're getting soaked.

She ducks inside, slams the door.

MARIANNE
(*awkward*)

Hi . . .

The car moves on.

LETOUR

Where are you going?

Marianne wipes rain from her cheeks; her expression deepens: cautious, suspicious. No reply.

I didn't know you still lived here.

MARIANNE
(*second thoughts*)

Maybe this wasn't such a good idea. I should get out.

LETOUR

Don't be crazy. It's pouring.

MARIANNE

I'm not supposed to be around –

LETOUR
(*completes sentence*)

– former drug associates.

MARIANNE

It's four years I'm clean. No alcohol, no cigarettes, no
nothing.

LETOUR

I heard. I'm happy for you.

MARIANNE

It's still not easy.

LETOUR

I know. Mar, you don't need to avoid me. I'm straight –
two years. It came that time. I tried to tell you. I wrote. I
called.

MARIANNE
(*looks around*)

I should get out.

LETOUR

Honest.

MARIANNE

But you're dealing.

LETOUR

No. I stopped.

MARIANNE

What's in the bag?

LETOUR

Almond oil. You can check.
(*opens bag*)

Look.

*She does: Enhancements Almond Oil. John's beeper goes off! – he
punches it.*

Shit.

MARIANNE

What's that for? In case someone needs almond oil in the middle of the night?

LETOUR

I still deal a little, but I'm straight – that part's true. Believe me.

MARIANNE
(*to driver*)

Stop here. Now. Stop!

LETOUR

I won't say anything. I promise. I'll just sit here. I'll just give you a ride.

The car pulls over. Marianne opens the door, gets out.

MARIANNE

Goodbye, John.

LETOUR

Where do you live?
(*door slams*)

Mari . . .

She fades into the rain. John watches, aching.

DRIVER

Sir?

LETOUR

83rd Street.

The sedan continues uptown.

CUT TO:

MEMORIES

John's apartment. Pre-dawn. His diary lies open on the desk. LeTour sits clothed on the futon, drinking white wine. He pages through a cheap, half-filled photo album. He touches snapshots, 3 by 5s from another time:

– John and Marianne, arm in arm, on a Florida beach

– Marianne, surprised by the camera, snorting coke at a party

– John, Marianne, and Ann posing, smiling, same party

– John and Marianne kissing over birthday cake, same party

– Marianne in Morocco bazaar

– John blowing a kiss in Fez airport.

    CUT TO:

PSYCHIC HEALING

LeTour's narration continues over embossed card on an entry table: Teresa Aronow, Psychic Reading, 37 Jones Street, New York, NY 10012, (212) 473–4297. Voices under narration:

                    TERESA (O.S.)

Coffee?

                    LETOUR (O.S.)

Thanks.

                    TERESA (O.S.)

Black?

                    LETOUR (O.S.)

Yeah.

                    TERESA (O.S.)

Here.

John accepts a coffee mug and sits on a sofa across from Teresa. Sunlight falls through crocheted curtains.

Teresa Aronow, fortyish, professionally young, is compact, demure; she wears business jacket and skirt, patterned blouse. Nothing about her is remotely paranormal – nothing except, of course, her 'aura.' The 'Other Side.' Her voice is at the same time soothing, piercing.

Teresa's West Village consultation room is startlingly mundane: a bourgeois walk-up. Upholstered furniture, Tiffany objêts d'art,

framed photos of her husband and children – a trip to Capri. A
twenties portrait of Madame Blavatsky, above the fireplace, centers
the room.

> LETOUR
>
> I'm not sure how this works.

> TERESA
>
> Have you ever been to a psychic before?

> LETOUR
>
> No, but I've, well, I've heard about it.

> TERESA
>
> Do you need advice? John?

> LETOUR
> (*nods*)
>
> No . . . it's not that . . . I don't know – I just decided to
> come. I thought . . .

> TERESA
>
> Be comfortable.
> (*smiles*)
> How did you hear about me?

> LETOUR
>
> A recommendation. Somebody from work. $200, right?

Teresa nods. John tucks cash into an envelope, places it on the coffee
table.

> TERESA
>
> It's a lot of money?

> LETOUR
>
> I don't care.

> TERESA
> (*explaining*)
>
> I look at you. I give you my impressions. I feel your 'vibra-
> tions' – I don't like that word, it sounds phony, but I can't
> think of anything better.

(*watching*)

You're anxious.

He shrugs.

More than usual. Your aura is very strong. I feel a very strong vibration from you. A change is coming. You're worried about money. You say you don't care about money, but that's not true.

LETOUR

Yeah.

TERESA

Your livelihood is endangered. You're worried about the future. You don't have much money saved. What will you do?

LETOUR

I don't know.

TERESA

I see a woman who has betrayed you.

LETOUR
(*smiles*)

My mother?

TERESA
(*cuts him short*)

Who *will* betray you.

LETOUR

Not . . . I . . .

TERESA

Keep it in mind. I have a strong feeling about this woman, a woman close to you, she will betray you. You're in the entertainment business, aren't you?

LETOUR

Yes.

TERESA

But you're not happy. You want to do something else. Is it
music?

LETOUR

Yes . . .

TERESA

You have a talent for music.

LETOUR

As a child.

TERESA

You still have it. It's strong. I see music in your future. A
career opportunity will come in the music field. Take it. It
won't seem promising. Take it anyway.
                              (*pause*)
You're full of stress. Are you exercising?

LETOUR

No. I –

TERESA

You should exercise more. You must let go of this stress.
It's not good for your health. I'm not saying you're going
over to the other side, but it's not good for you. You're still
drinking, aren't you? You have a drinking problem?

He shrugs.

It's interfering with your health and your life too. You've
had other problems. Drug addiction.

LETOUR

Yes.

TERESA

This was very important in your life.

LETOUR

Yes.

> TERESA

You are in the balance. Everything you do – positive or
negative – in this life is a drop that will carry over in the
next. Every act, every decision matters.

> LETOUR

Teresa?

> TERESA

What is it?

> LETOUR

I'm thirty-eight years old.
> (*beat*)
Forty.

> TERESA

You're young.

> LETOUR

I have trouble sleeping.

Teresa waits.

> Look. What do you see around me? Is there anything? Is it
> dark? Have I run out of luck? Is there luck?

> TERESA

I see a glow. Everything you need is around you. The only
danger is inside you.

CUT TO:

MONEY CHANGER

*Ann's apartment. The night has already begun. Ann sits on the floor
beside a young Hasid counting money. He wears Orthodox garb:
black hat, black coat, peyas. Tibetan bells reverb from speakers as
the Bergmanesque cambist runs faced twenty-dollar bills through a
battery-operated counting machine and places stacks of cash on the
floor. Robert returns a call from the kitchen; LeTour emerges from
the bathroom, wiping his hands.*

ANN
(*to LeTour and Robert*)
Your pay's on the table.

John walks to the cosmetics corner, finds an envelope with his name on it, looks inside: $500 in twenties. He pockets the money.

LeTour sits as Hasid double-checks the total: cash covers the available floor space.

YOUNG HASID
(*dialogue punctuates action*)
One hundred thirty-one, let's make it 130 – $13,000, hundreds for small bills. One per cent commission, $130 to you – add tens or whatever if you want.

Opening a satchel, he removes bound $100s, counts off 130 as Ann adds up commission in small bills. He loads the satchel:

Same time?

ANN
(*nods*)
Two weeks – don't run. Stay a while. We'll order kosher. We'll tell you dirty stories. We'll talk Zionism.

The Hasid laughs. He likes her.

YOUNG HASID
(*passes hundreds*)
I'm late already. I only come 'cause I like you. Sure you're not Jewish? I don't want to see you hurt. Find a man. You should do something else.

ANN
(*offers commission*)
Invest in my cosmetics line.

YOUNG HASID
(*takes money*)
Don't mix business with friendship.

Ann follows him to the door.

    Shalom.

ANN

    Shalom.
(*opens door*)

    See you next week.
(*calls after him*)

    Don't eat any hot dogs!

Ann closes door.

LETOUR

    Jealous said something about a yuppie murder in the Park. You know anything about it?

ANN

    It's all over the news.

LETOUR

    Jealous said to be careful.

ANN

    We are careful.

ROBERT
(*returning*)

    We're too small time. Besides, she wasn't one of ours – not directly.
(*to LeTour*)

    Tis is at St. Luke's. He wants somebody over right away. Second-floor waiting room.

LETOUR

    A hospital? What's he doing there?

ROBERT

    He says he needs you to come to St. Luke's. I'd go but I got the other thing.

LETOUR

    The –?

ROBERT

Yeah.

ANN
(*to LeTour*)
Go. Keep on his good side. He set up Arizona.

Phone rings; Ann's machine answers: 'Hello, this is Ann . . .'

(*to LeTour*)
Let's have lunch. Tomorrow.

LETOUR

Me?

ANN

One o'clock. Côte Basque. Is that too early?

LETOUR

No. Yeah – sure.

ROBERT

Tonight?

LETOUR

I vote Japanese.

ANN

Fine.

ROBERT

OK.

LETOUR
(*heads for door*)
Mixed sushi. Oshitashi.

CUT TO:

ST. LUKE'S

EMS vehicles line street outside St. Luke's–Roosevelt Hospital.
Inside, LeTour weaves through Emergency (eerie), double-steps the
stairs, looks for the second-floor waiting area.

*Tis (Mathis – pronounced Tees), thirty-five, Swiss, paces in the
waiting room. He wears a linen jacket, horn-rim glasses, Cerrutti
Euro-swank. He spots John and takes him aside.*

> LETOUR

What's going on?

> TIS

You got some valiums?

> LETOUR
> (*nods*)

– 'n 'ludes.

> TIS

Just a valium – a ten.

> LETOUR

What is it?

> TIS

You won't believe it. What a nightmare. I brought in this
chick. She OD'd – man, I didn't even know her. I didn't
have to bring her in. The cops are coming back to talk to
me. I'm hyper. I gotta come down.

> LETOUR
> (*hands him valium*)

Here.

> TIS

Make it two.

LeTour obliges. Tis pops a blue without water, pockets the other.

Thanks.

> LETOUR

She OK?

> TIS

Who?

LETOUR

The girl.

TIS

Yeah, yeah. Met her last night. A walking vacuum cleaner.
What a nightmare. Underage.

LETOUR

You need a lawyer?

TIS
(*gestures toward suited man*)
He's here. Thanks.

Tis folds a bill into John's hand.

LETOUR

Any time.

Tis turns, steps away. LeTour walks down the long corridor. Curious, reflective, he slows past open doors. Friends, family, patients sit in blue light. Each room a drama.

He heads down a duplicate corridor. A voice turns his head:

RANDI

John!

He turns to see Randi Jost, thirty, Marianne's younger sister. She wears running shoes, jeans, red sweater.

LETOUR

Randi?

RANDI
(*kisses him*)
I can't believe it. Marianne's here too. She flew in. It's
been so long. You look great.

LETOUR
(*deactivates beeper*)
You too. Randi, what's wrong? Why are you here?

RANDI

Mom. She's back in. Didn't Marianne tell you?

LETOUR

Serious?

RANDI
(*nods*)

More chemo.

LETOUR

Can I see her?

RANDI

She's sleeping. She sleeps most of the time. She'd like it, though. She still talks about you.

LETOUR
(*sad*)

I'm so sorry. She's a terrific woman. I was crazy about her. God.

Marianne, head down, approaches. Looking up, she finds herself unexpectedly beside John and Randi.

RANDI

It's John. What a coincidence.

MARIANNE
(*gathering herself*)

Yes.

(*extends hand*)

Hi.

LETOUR
(*shakes hand*)

Randi told me about your mom. I'm sorry.

MARIANNE

Thanks.

LETOUR

She's sedated?

MARIANNE

Yeah.

RANDI

She would be so happy to see John.

MARIANNE

I don't think that would be a good idea.

An awkward silence: Randi doesn't get it.

LETOUR

You both look so tired.

MARIANNE

One of us has to be here.

RANDI

The hospital lets us stay in her room.

LETOUR

Let me buy you some coffee or something – the cafeteria's downstairs. It helps to talk.

RANDI

You go, Marianne, it's my turn with Mom.

MARIANNE

I shouldn't.

RANDI

Go. You haven't eaten. Go on.
                         (*nudges her*)
Go on.

MARIANNE

I . . .

RANDI

Bring me a coffee.

Marianne acquiesces.

LETOUR

This way.

(*to Randi*)

Kiss your mother for me.

John escorts Marianne toward the stairs.

CUT TO:

EUPHORIC RECALL

Hospital cafeteria. John and Marianne carry trays to a formica table, molded chairs. He mixes sugar in his coffee as she sets out her salad, diet soda, to-go coffee.

An awkward moment. Marianne scans the fluorescent room: doctors, nurses, relatives.

LETOUR

I like your mom.

MARIANNE

She liked you. You know this will happen someday, but when it does . . . Your mother – *that* was a shock.

LETOUR
(*re: Marianne's mother*)

She's been sick a while?

MARIANNE

A year.

LETOUR

Your father?

MARIANNE
('*no*')

Not this time. His new wife – he'll make it to the funeral.

LETOUR

What have you been doing? Where do you live?

MARIANNE

It's . . .
(*deciding*)

I don't want you to know about my life.

LETOUR

Anything? You married? Have children? A dog?
(*smile*)
House plants?

MARIANNE

Details just open the door.

LETOUR

The door to what?
(*no answer*)
It's not like we're strangers. We were married.

MARIANNE

We were not.

LETOUR

There was a ceremony.

MARIANNE

He wasn't even a minister. He was an astrologer.

LETOUR

He was also a minister. 'Universal Harmony.'

MARIANNE

He was a Pisces.

LETOUR

You're a Pisces.

MARIANNE

It was *not* legal.

LETOUR

In the eyes of Jeanne Dixon we're still –

MARIANNE

I was on the cusp.

LETOUR

We were happy.

MARIANNE

We were miserable. We were either scoring or coming
down – mostly coming down.

LETOUR

There were good times. Area, out on the street, laughing,
dancing with friends – we were *magical*.

MARIANNE

You took off for three months without telling me and
called once. That's how magical we were. You were an
encyclopedia of suicidal fantasies – I heard them all.
Nobody could clear a room like you, John. And the
friends, you may have noticed, turned out to be mine, not
yours. I envy you. A convenient memory is a gift from
God.

LETOUR

You exaggerate.

MARIANNE

In rehab they call this 'euphoric recall.' You only remember the highs, never the lows.

LETOUR

We were happy.

MARIANNE

I was drowning.

LETOUR

It wasn't me –

MARIANNE

You watched –

LETOUR

You jumped –

MARIANNE

You did nothing – 'It wasn't your business, you weren't
responsible' – you still think like that.

                 (*shakes head*)
Actions have consequences; so do –

                  LETOUR
                  (*overlap*)
I –

                MARIANNE
– inactions.

                  LETOUR
I didn't –

Marianne smiles.

I meant well.

                MARIANNE
You always meant well.

                  LETOUR
We *were* in love?

                MARIANNE
Yes.

                  LETOUR
We *were* happy?

She doesn't answer. He slides his hand across the table. She notices his gold and onyx ring.

You bought it for me. It's inscribed inside.

She pushes his hand away. Details open doors.

Ann's quitting. I've got to find something else to do.

                MARIANNE
Ann? I'll believe it when I see it.

                  LETOUR
It's true.

                MARIANNE
Are you really straight?

                              LETOUR
Yeah.

                              MARIANNE
Let me see your eyes.

John leans forward, eyes open. She presses up an eyelid, examines one iris, the other.

        Eyes are deceiving.
                            (*beat*)
        Congratulations.

                              LETOUR
If I could do that, I could do anything.

                              MARIANNE
What do you mean?

                              LETOUR
We could do anything. We could start over.

                              MARIANNE
                         (*bangs her head*)
What was that? I think I heard something.

                              LETOUR
I'm serious.

An intercom voice announces visiting hours will end in five minutes.

                              MARIANNE
You're crazy.

                              LETOUR
                         (*gestures to room*)
This is crazy.

                              MARIANNE
I have to get back.

John nods, checks his watch – he's late too. They exchange 'last looks'; Marianne stands.

                              LETOUR
        I'll walk you.

He stands, follows.

        CUT TO:

NEW DIARY

*Later. LeTour's sedan pulls up near Palio, a midtown restaurant.
John steps around garbage bags, enters.*

Inside, John 'maps' bar, greets the maître d'. *LeTour spots the
French (LaCroix and Montana) couple in the dining section and
catches the man's eye. He nods to the* maître d' *and makes his way
toward their table.*

*He joins the French couple, declines a drink, and exchanges
drugs/money amid air kisses.*

*Late night. Fog hangs over 22nd Street: Chelsea's deserted. Homeless
men behind windbreaks of trash.*

*John's apartment. He writes bareback at the desk. He completes his
composition book diary mid-sentence, closes it, discards it. He lifts a
new book from the floor, opens it on the desk, continues. He fills his
glass with wine.*

                        LETOUR (V.O.)
        I can always find another way to make a living. I never
        planned this in the first place – not like Ann. She came up
        to sell, have parties, make contacts. She was so glamorous.
        I just wanted to be around her. She'd sit up listening to
        coke stories. Now it's me and Robert. The whole crowd
        was the same age. Everybody's younger now. She made
        me.

*LeTour pulls his weekly pay from his pants and puts five twenties in
an envelope. He addresses the envelope. 'Linda Wichel, 1012B-2 A
Street, Sacramento, California,' stamps it.*

*Dissolves: (1) LeTour vanishes from his desk, (2) materializes fetally
on his futon, bareback, slacks, boots, anxious, awaiting sleep.*

LeTour's diary contains parallel columns of names: one headed 'People Who Are Left Handed,' the other, 'People Whose Eyes Don't Match.'

CUT TO:

CÔTE BASQUE

Midday. John, wearing a black tweed jacket, tie, khaki slacks, mails the Sacramento letter, and then enters Côte Basque, a hoity-toity 55th Street restaurant.

Midmeal. Ann and LeTour sit in a prominent booth; power moguls confer quietly. A deferential waiter brings fresh berries and retrieves empty salmon plates.

ANN

You have any money saved?

LETOUR

There's some. Not much. A thousand or two. Maybe more – I'm not sure.

ANN

What do you do with your money?

The chef stops by and asks if the meal was satisfactory. Ann assures him it was and kisses his hand. The chef nods, gratified. John resumes the conversation.

LETOUR

I don't know. It's not that much in the first place – as you know.

ANN
(counterpoint)

It's tax-free –

LETOUR

Rent, utilities, phone, tips, CDs – what about your money?

ANN

Kitty Ford once told me, 'Ann, the only person I know
that lives as well as you is my grandmother.' All the money
I've made, all the money I've spent – it never adds up.
This last two years cosmetics' been taking everything.

LETOUR

I wish I could help.

ANN

You still go to meetings?

LETOUR

No, but I'm OK. What are the odds of meeting someone
you haven't seen in years twice in two days?

ANN

Ask Robert to make up a chart for you; the other person –
who is it?

LETOUR

Just a contact – you don't know him.

ANN

What's the plan?

LETOUR

The plan?

ANN

What you gonna do?

LETOUR

My future?

ANN

Too conceptual?

LETOUR

We had this conversation two years ago. We'll have it two
years from now.

ANN

This time it's for real.

> LETOUR
> (*accepting premise*)

I'm thinking of some music courses. Mixing, sound edit-
ing –

> ANN

You took that before.

> LETOUR

That was acting.

> ANN
> (*corrects him*)

Modeling.

> LETOUR

Why all this concern? Suddenly you care?

> ANN

I have feelings too – you may have noticed. I guess I'm
worried. I'm tough, you gotta to be tough, especially in
this business, it's one thing to act tough – I've seen Zippo-
rah twice this week.

> LETOUR

She helps you?

> ANN
> (*nods*)

– harmonizes, she's encouraging me to get out of this into
the cosmetics thing –

*Waiter leans in, deposits check as a well-tanned customer, fifty-five,
cologne and hauteur, passes. He looks at Ann blankly, continues. She
watches.*

> (*about customer*)

Nomination for Best Picture. I knew every girl he fucked –
how, why. I knew when he had trouble shitting. Like this.
> (*crosses fingers*)

His wife says he gets straight or she cuts him off. Old
money. I remember the last thing he said to me: 'See you

soon.' Yeah, sure. That was five years ago.

Ann pulls a wad of twenties from her purse and counts bills atop the check: $260.

>   (*vulnerable*)
> You'll still talk to me, won't you?

A beat: this is the reason for lunch. The waiter picks up the cash and appraises the gratuity.

>   LETOUR
> You –?
>   (*to Ann*)
> Of course I will.

>   ANN
> It'll be strange without you around. I hadn't thought of it
> – it hit me.

>   LETOUR
>   (*clever*)
> We'll always have Paris.

>   ANN
>   (*reproachful*)
> John.

John reaches, touches her visceral emotion. He takes her hand.

>   LETOUR
> Ann, you want me, call, write a letter, tell a wino – I'll be
> there.

She smiles, clasps his hand. Touching, he is touched.

>   CUT TO:

GENERAL HOSPITAL

Afternoon. St. Luke's. LeTour, wearing tweed jacket, walks down the corridor, checks room numbers. A nurse passes. He stops at a room, pushes the door a crack, peeks inside, and quietly enters.

Inside the hospital room, Mrs Jost, sixty-five, lies sedated, attached to IV tubes and a respirator. Flowers wreathe the bed.

Randi sleeps in a chair by the window.

LeTour looks from Mrs Jost to Randi and back again: a vibrant woman reduced to a shell. He soundlessly eases into a vacant chair.

His mind goes back.

Randi twists fitfully in her chair. A stuffed bear peeks over family photos on the window sill.

Marianne steps into the doorway, stops, frozen – watching the tableau: John, Randi, her mother. Her face is ravaged: the death watch has taken its toll. LeTour reaches his arm, touches the hospital bed.

Marianne tiptoes behind John. He turns, stands.

> LETOUR
> (*soft*)

I'm sorry. I . . .

She puts her finger to her lips. He nods. She steps closer, holds him politely. His cheek nestles in her neck. They turn toward the door, step into the corridor, walk arm in arm as if supporting each other.

> (*after a moment*)

I always thought my father would die first. He would die, then my mother and I would reconcile. Just her and me. I hated him for living.

> MARIANNE

It's like a joke. It's not a real feeling. It's like a feeling of a feeling.

> LETOUR

My old man bawling in the hospital, me popping in and out of the john getting loaded.

> (*beat*)

I miss you.

They stop. She kisses him.

                            MARIANNE
You tried to kill me. You took ten years of my life one way
or another.

He kisses her.

I couldn't hate my mom – I was too busy hating you.

                            LETOUR
I thought I was just killing myself.

She runs her hands under his shirt, up his back.

Selfish.

                            MARIANNE
I remember.

                            LETOUR
What?

                            MARIANNE
What it felt like.
                    (*kisses his face*)
What this tasted like.

He slips his hands under her blouse, caresses her breasts.

                            LETOUR
I see you and my heart starts thumping.

                            MARIANNE
John.

*They kiss deeper, bodies grinding. The painful present fades. A nurse
approaches with a wheelchair patient. She tries to pass one side of
John and Marianne, then tries the other side but is blocked again.
The nurse stops, stares at their soap opera.*

*Sensing her glare, John and Marianne, hands over and under each
other, stop and look to the nurse: embarrassed – yet blissful.*

                            LETOUR
Excuse us.

(*to Marianne*)

Let's go.

MARIANNE

Come. Come with me.

CUT TO:

HOTEL SEX

Paramount hotel room: Vermeer's Lace Maker *dominates Phillipe Starck decor.*

LeTour and Marianne are all over each other. The pain of the moment, the pain of the past are subsumed by passion. Blind, welcome sexuality.

Naked, they kneel facing each other on the bed, faded bleeding heart tattoo on his bicep.

LETOUR

Have you ever had sex totally straight?

MARIANNE

Not with you.

LETOUR

Neither have I.

MARIANNE

Such an erection.

LETOUR

Never had anything like it stoned. Feel it.

She does.

MARIANNE

Weird.

LETOUR
(*caresses erection*)

Wow.

MARIANNE

I'm dripping.

LETOUR

Let's disappear.

They smack their sweaty bodies, tumble yelping to the carpet, kiss indiscriminately.

Kiss, kiss, kiss.

MARIANNE

Kiss, kiss, kiss.

LETOUR

Together.

Later: night. They lie nude in a scramble of twisted sheets and mattresses. Street lights cast horizontal shadows.

LeTour crawls over, falls upon Marianne's breast. She wakes up, looks at John, looks out the window, and returns to slow sad reality.

Marianne stands and pulls on her panties.

(*waking*)
You need to go back?

She dresses before responding.

MARIANNE

This is the end. It was wonderful. I'm glad it happened this way. It will never happen again. You will not see me, you will not call me again. I'm happy for you. I wish you the best. I'm leaving. I'm going back to the hospital. I shouldn't have left – but I don't regret it. Please dress and leave as soon as possible. I have a key. Goodbye.

LETOUR

Marianne . . .

MARIANNE

It's my fault.

Marianne, clothes askew, exits.

LETOUR

I love you.

LeTour is alone. He pulls his pants on. Looking for his socks, he peruses Marianne's personal things. He examines her cosmetics, her underclothes. He dabs her perfume on his cheek.

Buttoning his shirt, he retrieves his beeper from his suit jacket. Activated, it disgorges messages. He checks his watch: 9.00 p.m.

CUT TO:

GET ON OUT

9.30 p.m.: Ann's apartment building. Trash stacked high.

LeTour presses the buzzer.

LeTour, exhausted, unfocused, enters Ann's apartment. Ann is immediately upon him:

ANN

Johnny, what is this? Your beeper broke, gettin' some shi-atsu? Two hours: where have you been?

LETOUR

There was a mix-up –

ANN

How you gonna survive on your own? The UN's got some conference in two days. The holiday's over – ragheads everywhere trying to score. UN security at every hotel – little creeps with lapel pins. Even I've been out. This is where our money is: Europe, Asia, not the streets – you wouldn't know crack from crackerjacks.

LETOUR

Where's Robert?

ANN

Busting his ass. He's out doing your job.

LETOUR

It was a confusion.

ANN

Get confused on your day off.

LETOUR

When is that?

ANN

Don't get wise. What do you want me to do? Suck your
dick? – OK. A raise? No way. Get out there. There's a list
on the TV. I love you. Get your ass outta here before I kiss
it.

LETOUR
(*pecks her cheek*)
I'm on my way. Love you. Forgive me.

CUT TO:

AU BAR

LeTour's sedan waits between limos.

Inside, John passes the maître d' *and looks around: he's known
here. Au Bar, a restaurant/club open 9.00 p.m. to 4.00 a.m., caters
to the young, the rich, the European.*

*He spots Tis with Thomas, twenty-five, his handsome trainer, and
two models at a second-floor table. They exchange nods. LeTour
scans the room: suspicion is second nature.*

*A laughing man (Guidone) at the bar catches his eye. He seems to
blend: Italian, twenty-eight, silk suit, impeccable hair, accent – but
something's not right. His black shoes have rubber soles. LeTour
looks for a gun bulge, dirty hands. The Italian turns; LeTour
glimpses his face: too pale. The Italian averts his eyes. Glancing
back, LeTour walks up the stairs to Tis's table.*

TIS

Tour, sit. Take a rest. LeTour, this is Gabri, Tasha – you
know Thomas. They're here for a show.

*The models respond in respective accents. Thomas extends his hand.
John shakes, but remains standing.*

LETOUR

Enchanté.
                    (*to Tis*)
How'd it turn out?

TIS
                    (*to Gabri*)
Questo è un vero Americano.
                    (*to LeTour*)
What?

Gabri and Tasha buzz.

LETOUR

St. Luke's.

TIS

No problem, but – can you believe this? – she's out of the
hospital in one day, calls me up, wants to 'get together.'
Some people are just born for losing. Want to go in back?

LETOUR

Not now.

TIS

Huh?

LETOUR

Look at the bar. Black-haired guy, late twenties, brown
suit, drinking tonic?

Tis nods.

He's casing you. Not me, you. Undercover, whatever –
he's on you.

TIS

You know him?

LETOUR
                    (*shakes head 'no'*)
Just a feeling. You holding?

TIS

No. Need help?

LETOUR
(*'no'*)

Leave a message. Robert or I will come by later.

TIS

Forget it. It wasn't for me anyway.
(*to models*)
Who am I trying to impress?

They smile uncomprehendingly.

Make it tomorrow. A half – no, three-quarters.

LETOUR

Nineteen is the top. I'll make two trips.

TIS

Nineteen is fine.

LETOUR
(*leaving*)

A domani. Take care, girls.

CUT TO:

THERE IS A DIRECTION

The blue sedan drives west past Times Square, turns north on 8th Avenue. A plastic wall of trash stretches toward the river. Port Authority hustlers – male, female – cruise as transit cops whack an emaciated crackhead. John, lit by neon, lowers his power window.

John's apartment. Night. He writes in his diary and drinks.

LETOUR (V.O.)

I feel my life turning. All it needed was a direction. You drift from day to day, years go by. Suddenly there is a direction. What a strange thing to happen halfway through your life.

He goes to the phone, dials. A voice answers.

HOTEL SWITCHBOARD (O.S.)
Paramount Hotel.

LETOUR
Marianne Jost, please.

HOTEL SWITCHBOARD (O.S.)
Just a moment.

A pre-recorded message comes on:

HOTEL MESSAGE
'Welcome to the Paramount. Your party is out. If you
would like to leave a message for –'
(*Marianne's voice*)
'Marianne Jost –'
(*back to message*)
'– please do so after the beep.'

*LeTour hangs up, carries the phone to the boombox. He dials again,
presses 'Record,' holds the receiver to the mike, records the hotel message, hangs up.*

*First light slants from the window. LeTour lies clothed on the futon,
boombox by his ear. He presses 'Play' and 'Rewind,' running the
tape over and over, listening, re-listening to Marianne's voice: 'Marianne Jost.' 'Marianne Jost.' 'Marianne Jost.'*

CUT TO:

PHONE CALLS

*Midday. 22nd Street. A helter-skelter of daytime activity unseen
before.*

*John's apartment. Sunlight fills the studio apartment. LeTour,
unshaven in T-shirt and slacks, sets the phone on the desk beside his
open composition book. He pauses, then dials.*

HOTEL SWITCHBOARD (O.S.)
Paramount Hotel.

> LETOUR

Marianne Jost.

> HOTEL SWITCHBOARD (O.S.)

Just a moment.

John waits, closes his diary.

I'm sorry. Ms Jost checked out this morning.

> LETOUR

She was there yesterday.

> HOTEL SWITCHBOARD (O.S.)

She checked out this morning.

> LETOUR

Did she leave a forwarding number?

> HOTEL SWITCHBOARD (O.S.)

No.

> LETOUR

Thank you.

He hangs up, thinks, redials.

> ST. LUKE'S SWITCHBOARD (O.S.)

St. Luke's–Roosevelt Hospital.

> LETOUR

Mrs Jost. JoAnn Jost. She's a patient.

> ST. LUKE'S SWITCHBOARD (O.S.)

Just a moment.

A long silence. John looks out the window. A medical staff voice from the hospital:

> MEDICAL VOICE (O.S.)

Who is this calling?

> LETOUR
> (*thinking*)

Skyline Floral. We're trying to confirm a delivery.

MEDICAL VOICE (O.S.)
Mrs Jost passed away last night.

LETOUR
Are the funeral arrangements local?

MEDICAL VOICE (O.S.)
Just a sec – yes, Plaza Memorial.

LETOUR
Thank you.

MEDICAL VOICE (O.S.)
You're welcome.

John hangs up, paces, sits.

CUT TO:

DIRTY LAUNDRY

Afternoon. Chelsea laundromat. Mothers and maids gossip, sort clothes. Hispanic radio underscores the whirl of machines. LeTour, unshaven, shoves dirty clothes into a washer. He counts out quarters and starts the machine.

Heading toward a vacant chair, he spots a man out the window. It takes a second to place the face: it's the 'Italian' from Au Bar in street clothes. He watches John watching him. LeTour walks outside and approaches Guidone on the sidewalk.

LETOUR
Can I help you, officer?

GUIDONE
What?

LETOUR
I hope I haven't made a mistake. You are a cop, aren't you?

GUIDONE
Yes.

                            LETOUR
Could I see a badge?

*Guidone eyes LeTour with disdain: the contempt of a cop for a
dealer, of youth for middle age.*

                            GUIDONE
                        (*shows credentials*)
Bill Guidone.

                            LETOUR
What is it?

                            GUIDONE
You think you're invisible, don't you? You think we don't
know you, LeTour – that's the name you use, right?

                            LETOUR
My father's a partner in a powerful law firm. If you have
anything in mind, do it by the book.

*Guidone elbow-stabs LeTour and kicks his shin. Wincing, retreating,
John staggers, then regains his balance.*

                            GUIDONE
                        (*in his face*)
You? Who the fuck cares about you? I could grind you
right here! – maybe I will! – and nobody would give a
fuck! You're not worth the paperwork. I look like Nar-
cotics? I'm Homicide – I'm investigating the Park murder.

                            LETOUR
                        (*acquiescent*)
I don't follow the news.

                            GUIDONE
Downtown's interested how a Barnard honors student
with fancy parents got a quarter of uncut coke on her
when she was murdered. I mean, we just don't see this girl
cruising Alphabet City trying to score. Somebody sold
her, somebody upscale and classy – you're classy, I hear –

and that somebody knows something we need to know.
(*hand inside LeTour's shirt, pinching his tit*)
Delivery boy!

LETOUR

I wish I could help. I don't even know who's president.

GUIDONE

Let me put it this way. Here's my card.
(*hands card*)
Ask around, take a week or so. Call me. Tell me something
I don't know. Either that, leave town, or get your ass
busted day in, day out.

LeTour examines the card.

CUT TO:

FUNERAL HOME

*Evening. LeTour, shaven, in black tweed jacket, white shirt, black
tie, crosses Amsterdam Avenue and enters Plaza Memorial
Chapel.*

*Inside the funeral home, John checks the letterboard for Mrs Jost's
name. An arrow directs him.*

*Non-denominational muzak. Senior citizens whisper off-screen.
Walking, he sees Marianne, dressed in black. She sees him and turns
to him; her face hollow, desperate.*

MARIANNE

Get out.

LETOUR

Marianne . . .

MARIANNE
(*emotion rising*)
Every time you come into my life something terrible happens. I thought I was rid of you. How'd you get here? I
don't want you here! I don't want you around me, I don't

want you around my mother! Đamn you!

LETOUR

Marianne . . .

MARIANNE
(wild)

Get out!

A plaza memorial employee approaches. Randi, in black, intervenes, pulls John toward the door. Marianne yells from behind: 'Out!' Outside, they stop mid-sidewalk.

LETOUR

I didn't . . .

RANDI

I'm sorry. That's the way it is. You shouldn't have come. Marianne has been up all night, crying and crying. She wasn't there when Mother passed – died – she blames herself. It wouldn't have made any difference. She just slipped away. Marianne's – I'm worried –

A crackhead strides past trash ramparts, cursing, demanding money: 'Fuck white devil, fucking the black, give the fucking money, white fuck . . .,' etc.

LETOUR

It's . . .

RANDI

Don't try.

LETOUR

How are *you*?

RANDI

Me?

LETOUR

Yes, you. I can't think of anything, but if there was anything I could do . . .

RANDI

Thanks. I'm OK – I guess. I mean, we've been expecting
it. It'll hit me later.

LETOUR

I saw her.

RANDI

Who?

LETOUR

Your mother. I came in the room. You were sleeping. I just
watched.

RANDI

Oh.
(*beat*)
I'd better get back. Marianne's probably flipping out.

She re-enters the funeral chapel.

CUT TO:

ON A ROLL

*8 p.m. LeTour, direct from Plaza Memorial, enters Ann's apart-
ment. Ann, coiffured and made up, gestures to take-out tins.*

ANN

Have some shu mai. Just delivered.

LETOUR

No.

ROBERT
(*entering*)

I told Ann you'd be on time. Tis called. He said before
ten. He said you were right.

ANN

About what?

LETOUR

An undercover cop. Not a narc. The Park murder. Jealous

was straight on that – you hear anything?

ROBERT

Remember the time that cop called here? Wanted to know if we had 'nose candy'?
(*laughs*)
Ann says, 'John Candy?' 'John Candy?'

Ann looks at John and approaches.

ANN

What's wrong baby? You look like shit. Something wrong?

She holds LeTour's face.

LETOUR

No.

ANN

You can't fool me. I can read you.

LETOUR
(*distressed*)

What do you care? You're leaving me. A few more months – *sayonara*.
(*to Robert*)
You too. John who? What was his name again? Le –?
(*to Ann: pained*)
I mean, it's not exactly like I got a pension plan.

ROBERT
(*hurt*)

Jack.

ANN
(*takes his hands*)

Johnny, it's not that at all. Is that what you think? You *hate* cosmetics. You don't care about it. You *told* me that.

LETOUR

I know.

> ANN

Who knows what will happen?

> ROBERT

I got a friend – a D.D. – got into lapidary. I'll introduce
you. You have to pass a test.

> LETOUR

Lapi –?

> ROBERT

Gems, you know, crystals, diamonds.

> LETOUR

Any more about the Park murder?

> ANN
> (*re: murder*)

What's with this thing?

> ROBERT

Stay away.

> ANN
> (*genuine*)

You want in? We'll make a place for you.

> LETOUR

No.

> ANN

It's –

The kitchen phone rings. A voice follows the pre-recorded message:

> EDDIE (O.S.)
> (*answering machine*)

'Ann, this is Ed. You gotta come. The other thing is over.
I'll be home all night. 749-2876.'

> ROBERT

Shit.

> ANN
> (*unequivocal*)
>
> Don't answer it. Let him call all night. He's trouble. I
> don't want to deal with him.

> LETOUR
>
> It's all right, I'll go. Let me handle it.

> ROBERT
>
> I'm sorry if –

> ANN
> (*about Eddie*)
>
> He gives you shit – fuck him.

> LETOUR
> (*to Robert*)
>
> Forget it.

> ROBERT
>
> We're going Chinese tonight, OK? I mean we're on a roll –

> ANN
>
> Spring roll.

> LETOUR
> (*preparing to leave*)
>
> Sure, whatever. Surprise me.

CUT TO:

INTERVENTION

Eddie's high-rise apartment. Eddie is worse, if anything. He's been scoring on the street: broken pipes and vials crunch underfoot.

Eddie and LeTour argue ('Fuck you!' 'Fuck you!'). Eddie spits, pushes Tour; John pushes back. Eddie's feet tangle. He trips, falls. A bottle smashes.

John goes to the phone, checks Eddie's directory, and dials.

EDDIE
(*on floor*)
You gotta get permission? Check with Mama?

LETOUR
I'm calling your brother.

EDDIE
Huh?

LETOUR
Yeah, the lawyer in Bronxville. I'm gonna ask him to come over.

Eddie protests.

You've told me so much about him.

EDDIE
(*panicked*)
No, don't. Please, I'll give you money, anything. He doesn't understand. Whose side are you on?

LETOUR
(*on phone*)
Is this Martin Jeer?
(*beat*)
Thank you.

Eddie, woozy, tries to stand.

EDDIE
I shoulda never called.

LETOUR
(*to Eddie*)
I recommend Hazelden. It has the best all-around program.
(*on phone*)
Martin Jeer?
(*beat*)
I'm here with your brother Ed.

(*beat*)

Yeah, in the city. I'm afraid there's a medical emergency. You're going to have to come.

Eddie lurches toward LeTour. John – flash of anger – boot-kicks him in the head! Eddie's cheek hits the carpet.

(*on phone*)

He'll be here.

John, cooling down, measures his breaths. A spring can only be wound so tight.

CUT TO:

LEXINGTON AVENUE

LeTour walks from his sedan around the corner to the Lexington Avenue entrance to Grace Towers, a pre-war apartment building.

In the lobby, he gives his name to the security guard and is directed to the express elevator.

He exits on the thirtieth floor; footsteps muted by thick carpet. Victorian prints on dark blue walls. He looks about, approaches a door, and presses the buzzer.

Thomas opens the door; John enters Tis's opulent apartment. Salle and Clemente hang on the walls; New York twinkles outside panoramic windows. A pipe and syringe lie atop art books.

Tis, in jogging sweats, comes from the bedroom to greet him.

TIS

Tour, just in time. We were out. Nineteen, right?

LETOUR

Thirty-eight hundred – got any hundreds?

TIS

Some, not the whole thing.

(*to Thomas*)

You got hundreds?

THOMAS

No.

LeTour hands him a plastic bag of gram envelopes. Tis opens a packet, pours the contents on the coffee table.

TIS

I like that about Ann. Always takes the time to grind it. If you do it, do it right.

John hears footsteps, turns to see Marianne stumble out of the bedroom! She looks terrible: shoeless, blouse out, hair undone, bruise on her forehead – perhaps she fell against something – hands trembling.

(*to Marianne*)
Looks like you could use some help.

Marianne looks up, sees John, goes pale.

Mari, this is Tour. You got any hundreds?

John stares speechless: the girl who won't talk to him because he's a dealer. Marianne bolts back into the bedroom, slams the door!

Not the talkative type. Haven't seen her in years. You know her, don't you?

No answer. Tis counts the money, offers it. LeTour is frozen.

Why they call me? What a nightmare.
(*extending money*)
You want it or not?

LETOUR
(*vacant*)
Yeah.

LeTour pockets the cash. Tis, his arm on John's elbow, 'walks' him to the door.

TIS

See you later.

Tis nudges John to the corridor and closes the door behind him. John looks toward the elevator; Tis, behind the door, calls, 'Marianne!'

Timecut: LeTour stands in the elevator, red floor numbers flashing past, blank eyes mirrored in dark glass.

CUT TO:

FALL FROM GRACE

John exits Grace Towers, walks past a limo toward Lexington Avenue. Rounding the corner, he sees his blue sedan. He looks at the cash, repockets it. He continues slowly, each step a separate task.

LeTour reaches for the door handle. A scream pierces traffic noise. A car screeches, another. Voices call out.

LeTour steps back, listens. He retraces his steps, turns on to Lexington Avenue. The security guard, walkie-talkie in hand, clusters on the sidewalk with the limo driver and two pedestrians. A cabbie jumps from his taxi, joining the confusion ('My God!'). A siren approaches. John's beeper goes off.

Drawing closer, LeTour sees the partial bloodied shape of a broken body on the sidewalk: he recognizes Marianne's skirt. A squad car brakes with a screech. Two cops converge, climb over trash, and clear the crime scene.

> FEMALE COP

Get back!

> MALE COP

Who saw it? What happened?

The female cop bends over Marianne's body.

EMS is on the way.

> FEMALE COP

Too late –

A second squad car pulls up. John turns away, walks around the corner.

LeTour opens the car door, closes it, sits inside. A wailing ambulance flashes past, speeds up Central Park West. LeTour doesn't react. Beeper re-beeps; he disconnects the battery.

The driver, Carlos, twenty-five, Hispanic, shirt starched, turns,
looks, thinks, says:

> CARLOS

Where to?

> LETOUR

What?

> CARLOS

Where to, sir? Where are we going?

> LETOUR

Nowhere just now. Wait.

> CARLOS
> *(after a moment)*

You want me to wait here?

> LETOUR

Yes.

Pause. More police cars. The EMS siren starts up; the ambulance
speeds downtown past LeTour's sedan. No reaction. Carlos turns off
the engine.

Downtown.

> CARLOS

Yes.

Carlos starts the car and pulls into traffic.

CUT TO:

TWENTY-TWO MINUTES

John's apartment. Late night. LeTour, barefoot, T-shirt, slacks,
stands flat against the wall.

WINS broadcasts twenty-four-hour news on the boom box. ('Give
us twenty-two minutes and we'll give you the world.') Sports, ads,
bullshit – LeTour hears what he's been waiting for.

NEWSCASTER (O.S.)
(*on radio*)

This story is just in. A woman has fallen thirty stories to her death from a posh Grace Towers apartment on Lexington Avenue. Police are withholding identification pending the notification of the next of kin. The incident happened about 10 p.m. According to the sources on the scene there was no one else in the posh Grace Towers apartment when the fall occurred. We will bring you more details as we get them.

(*teletype efx*)

An end to the sanitation strike seems imminent. Negotiations at the Helmsley Palace are continuing to this hour . . .

Actions have consequences.

CUT TO:

MOTHER TERESA

First light. Jones Street. LeTour, sleepless, pounds on Teresa's door. No answer. Knocks again. Again.

Noises from inside. A sleepy voice:

TERESA (O.S.)
Who is it?

LETOUR
John. John LeTour. Can I see you?

TERESA (O.S.)
What time is it?

LETOUR
It's important, Teresa.

TERESA (O.S.)
Call. Make an appointment.

LETOUR
Open the door. You're awake anyway.

No answer.

Teresa.

Teresa, wearing oriental bathrobe, unlatches the door. John enters and turns to her. The door closes.

Read me. What do you see?

TERESA

Do I know you?

LETOUR

We had a session last week. What do you see?

TERESA
(*remembering name*)

John?

LETOUR

Yes. Look at me.

Teresa takes a moment to concentrate.

TERESA

Step back.

He does.

Again.

He does.

Death.

LETOUR

Someone I knew died tonight.

TERESA

This was not an accident. This person was murdered.

LETOUR

Am I in danger?

TERESA
(*beat*)

There is danger around you. It's very close. I'm sleepy.

LETOUR
What should I do?

TERESA
I can't see it.

LETOUR
Please.

She shrugs.

Am I lucky?

TERESA
Yes. Don't be afraid. Go home.

Teresa shuffles toward her bedroom – the 'reading' is over.

LETOUR
What do I owe you?

TERESA
Nothing. Forget it. Let me sleep.

CUT TO:

SNITCH

Mid-morning. LeTour, still awake, walks past towering Chelsea trash.

He passes a news-stand. Tabloids feature yearbook photo of Marianne; the headline: 'FALL FROM GRACE.' LeTour walks to a payphone, takes out Guidone's card, inserts a quarter, and dials.

POLICE SWITCHBOARD (O.S.)
Ninth Precinct.

LETOUR
Bill Guidone, please. Homicide.

POLICE SWITCHBOARD (O.S.)
Hold on.

John, suspicious, looks around. Guidone speaks:

GUIDONE (O.S.)

Guidone.

LETOUR

This is John LeTour. Remember me?

GUIDONE (O.S.)

Laundromat. Your father's got connections.

LETOUR

You said I should ask around, tell you something you
didn't know.

GUIDONE (O.S.)

I thought you'd call.

LETOUR

It ain't much, but it's something.

GUIDONE (O.S.)

Go on.

LETOUR

A girl died last night. Lexington Avenue.

GUIDONE (O.S.)

The jumper. Druggie.

LETOUR

The news said she was alone in the apartment when she went
out – she wasn't. It's a cover-up. There was someone else.

GUIDONE (O.S.)

Who?

LETOUR

Who lives in the apartment?

GUIDONE (O.S.)

You there?

LETOUR

That's all I know. You asked me to tell you something. I
told you something.

He hangs up.

    CUT TO:

A LITTLE SLEEP

Noon. LeTour enters a West Village apartment building. He presses an intercom button. Robert's voice answers:

                          ROBERT (O.S.)
    Who is it?

                          LETOUR
    Jack. Let me in.

The door buzzes.

Robert opens the door to his overdecorated apartment. John looks around. Tony, Robert's younger, unattractive lover, sips coffee at the table.

                          ROBERT
    Where have you been? We were worried.

                          LETOUR
    I need some sleep – not much. I don't want to go home just yet. A little sleep first. Can I crash here? Nice place.

                          ROBERT
    It's hideous. I did it years ago. I've got to throw everything out. You haven't been here?
                      (*noticing Tony*)
    Oh, Jack, this is Tony. I told you about him. You should talk. He's the lapidopterist – gems.

                          TONY
                      (*corrects him*)
    Lapidarian.

                          ROBERT
    Same thing.

                          LETOUR
    Can I?

ROBERT

Sure.

LETOUR

What do you know about Tis? What's his relationship to
Ann?

ROBERT

They go way back – before me. Did you cross him?

LETOUR

No.

ROBERT

Don't. He's Ann's Ecstasy connection. She needs that
score. What happened?

LETOUR

Nothing.

ROBERT

Don't mess with him.

LETOUR

Is he dangerous?

ROBERT

Everybody's dangerous. We heard what you did to Eddie.
Ann thought it was great. She was afraid that was why you
didn't come back.

LETOUR

It was something else. Tell me if you hear anything.

ROBERT

About what?

LETOUR

Tis.

ROBERT

Tis who? Ann says you want a chart done.
                    (*beat*)
What's wrong?

LETOUR
(*internal*)

Ah . . .

ROBERT
(*sympathetic*)

You down?

LETOUR
(*nods*)

Yeah . . .
(*culling thoughts*)
You ever think about it?

ROBERT

What?

LETOUR

That it'd be like this – like, your life, you . . . that it would
turn out this way? –

ROBERT

Compared to what? My thinking this or that is going to
make any difference? There's a plan unfolding. 'Will my
plane crash?' 'Does life have meaning?' – why ask me?
Thinking's a fear of living, negative living; living's something else. You're afraid. Let the plan unfold. Stop. Stop,
live one day – one day –

Words blur to jargon. LeTour cuts in:

LETOUR

– Robert –

ROBERT

– day at a time.

LETOUR
(*touches Robert*)

You've lost your fucking brain.

> ROBERT
> (*laughs*)

I'm a drug dealer.

> LETOUR

Got a tub?

> ROBERT
> (*gestures*)

Yeah.

> LETOUR

Great.

Turns to bathroom.

> ROBERT

There's a plastic bottle of bath oil in the cabinet. Yellow.
Use it – tell me what you think. It's a new formula.

CUT TO:

JUMP-OFFS

*6 p.m. LeTour, shaved and bathed, rides a cab uptown, past
Harlem, past 158th Street. He motions to the driver; the taxi stops at
a blue door between retail stores begging for renovation.*

Teenage Latinos hang out. LeTour gives the cabbie a twenty.

*LeTour walks to the blue door; the youths stop, watch. He knocks on
the door. A Puerto Rican doorman in white leather pants and a
heart-shaped diamond ring opens the door and looks him over.
John reaches into his pouch, removes a gram envelope, hands it to
him. The doorman takes a taste, buzzes him through a door hand-
lettered 'Jump-Offs.'*

*Inside Jump-Offs, a cocaine 'spot,' every eye turns to John: the only
Anglo in a Hispanic after-hours club. Tough young faces, each with
a style and two inches of attitude. Willie Colon plays on the jukebox.*

Searching, LeTour recognizes a face and walks over.

LETOUR

Manny.

Manuel, thirtyish, Puerto Rican, looks closer, trying to place LeTour.

LeTour.
                    (*helping out*)
Jealous. 'Jell.' SOBs.

MANUEL
(*remembering*)

Reggae night.

LETOUR

Burning Spear.

MANUEL

How'd you get in?

LETOUR

C-C.

MANUEL

You buying?

LETOUR

How's product?

MANUEL
(*gesture: 'primo'*)

How much?

LETOUR

I got a problem. I need a piece.

MANUEL

Piece? Piece of what? Piece of candy?

LETOUR

A gun.

MANUEL

When?

LETOUR
Now. Anything.

Manuel is silent.

Am I speaking too fast?

MANUEL
How much you spend?

LETOUR
The rate. What you got?

Manuel calls over a teenage Dominican, explains the situation in Spanish. The Dominican replies; Manuel turns back to John.

MANUEL
He's got a 64 Smithson. Detective Special. Nobody wants 'em. Fresh from a cop.

LETOUR
How much?

MANUEL
(*consults Dominican*)
Four – including me.

LETOUR
You're fucking me.

MANUEL
(*'so what?'*)
Street price.

LETOUR
Where is it?

MANUEL
Sigame.

They lead him to an even darker back room.

The Dominican retrieves an automatic pistol from a trash pail and hands it to Manuel. John counts cash from Tis's roll; Manny hefts the piece.

The hundreds – Franklins.

Bills and guns exchanged.

> LETOUR

How do you use this?

> MANUEL

Automatic.

> LETOUR

I don't have much use for a gun. Never used one like this.

> MANUEL
> (*translates for Dominican*)

Coño!

The Dominican laughs; LeTour takes his measure.

> LETOUR
> (*businesslike*)

What do you do?

> MANUEL

Simple. You put the bullets in –
> (*inserts cartridge*)

– you point it at the bad guys, pull the trigger, and they fall down!

Manny repeats this for the Dominican ('bang, bang!'); they laugh again. LeTour eases the .38 into his crotch. Manny turns, exchanges a Latin hug.

Vaya con Dios.

> LETOUR

– Dios.

John exits and works his way through the club.

CUT TO:

OUT WITH THE OLD

John's apartment. 7 p.m. LeTour, sweating, bareback, tucks the .38 under his futon.

He takes a bottle of cologne from the bathroom, pours it over his hair, face, and torso, and rubs it in.

Licking his finger, he removes Marianne's gold and onyx ring with a tug. His finger stings. He opens a window, throws the ring full force into the junk-strewn courtyard. He shakes his torso; cologne glistens.

CUT TO:

JOHN AND RANDI

Interior, Plaza Memorial Chapel. LeTour enters the 'viewing room' and motions to Randi. She follows him.

They slip into a door and enter the embalming room: stainless-steel table surrounded by surgical cabinets.

They embrace, disengage. John looks: Randi's exhausted face mirrors his.

> LETOUR
> Have you been to the police station?

> RANDI
> (*nods*)
> She was back on drugs. Really back. They're gonna bring her here too. My God.

He comforts her.

> I thought she was playing for attention.

> LETOUR
> I didn't know.

> RANDI
> You're not to blame. Don't blame yourself. You weren't responsible. She was always – she loved you.

LETOUR

(*wipes tear from her cheek*)

She loved you. You were what she wanted to be.

RANDI

She scared me.

John pulls a Polaroid from his pocket.

LETOUR

Look. Do you recognize anyone?

The picture features Ann and Tis: side by side at a dinner party.

RANDI

Tis.

LETOUR

You know him?

RANDI

His father's a lawyer. Did some tax things for Mom. He was at the hospital. What's that smell?

LETOUR

It's me. Cologne. I'm a sucker for that cheap airplane stuff. Did Marianne mention him yesterday?

RANDI

(*'no'*)

It was his apartment. What are you thinking?

LETOUR

I don't know.

RANDI

She jumped.

LeTour hangs on every word.

You loved her, but she – this sounds terrible but it's true – she was . . . she ruined everything . . . bad luck.

                              LETOUR
                          (*heard enough*)
When's the funeral – your mother's?

                              RANDI
Tomorrow. Will you come?

                              LETOUR
                            (*vague*)
Well, I got this thing to do. It's – I don't know if I can get
away.

                              RANDI
Try? For me.

                              LETOUR
I'll try.

CUT TO:

PRODIGAL SON

Ann's apartment. 8 p.m. Ann greets LeTour with a hug.

                              ANN
The Prodigal Son.

                              LETOUR
Sorry about last night. Something came up.

                              ANN
Where were you?

                              LETOUR
T.C.T.E.

                              ROBERT
'Too Complicated To Explain.'

                              LETOUR
                          (*enters bedroom*)
I'm $500 short from last night. I'll get it, you can take it
from my salary.

ANN
(*stung*)
This is family. Are you saying that to hurt me?

Le Tour returns.

It's not money.

LETOUR
(*chagrined*)
Sorry.

ROBERT
Look at this.

'Akasha' visual.

We had a graphic artist make it up – you know, Billy, Five
Towns.

ANN
The label for the cosmetics line.

LETOUR
(*examines it*)
Classy. Sorta – Katmandu . . .

ANN
(*corrects him*)
*Kath*mandu.

LETOUR
I love it.

ROBERT
Tis called twice. He wants you to come by.

LETOUR
(*wary*)
Me?

ANN
Yeah. Says you were supposed to show up again yesterday,
but didn't.

LETOUR

A lie. I don't want to go. The suicide and all. Let's stay
away.

ANN

Can't. He's the Ecstasy connect. No way I can fuck this.

LETOUR

C'mon . . .

ANN

This is business.

*LeTour, suspicious, looks from Ann to Robert. He knows Tis knows
he knows Marianne was not alone when she went out the window.*

LETOUR

Let Robert go.

ANN

Tis won't deal with fags.

LETOUR

Since when?

ANN

Just is – so he's a bigot? What's new? So's everybody else.

LETOUR

I don't want to go. I got a bad vibe.

ROBERT

He said you.

ANN
(*to LeTour*)

Why?

LETOUR
(*to Ann*)

Why don't you go? He's *your* contact.

ROBERT

He is –

> ANN
> (*to Robert*)
>
> You giving orders?

> ROBERT
> (*deferential*)
>
> No, missy.

> LETOUR
> (*testing her*)
>
> Come with me – the two of us.

> ANN
> (*upbeat*)
>
> OK. You got it. Like old times – Ann and Johnny.

She turns to go.

> LETOUR
>
> OK.

> ROBERT
>
> Stop it. You're breaking my heart.

CUT TO:

LAST RIDE

Night. Ann and LeTour side by side in the sedan. Carlos at the wheel, anonymous. Outside, sanitation workers toss sacks of trash into garbage trucks: the strike is over.

Ann reminisces as lights flash.

> ANN
>
> It's going to be strange, not doing this. I mean I've had it, but sometimes . . .

> LETOUR
>
> You're gonna do it, aren't you? You're gonna quit.

> ANN
> (*nods*)
>
> I think so. Seal this thing with Tis, turn it – go with the

cosmetics. You gotta take a chance in life. No risk, no
gain. I've already got retail connections here, London. It
was great at the beginning, though.

LETOUR

When?

ANN

You know, when we first started out of the place on
Greene Street. Before deliveries, when you were still
using. It was open house every night but Sunday. We had
everything: uppers, downers, meth, six kinds of hash, all in
that trousseau, remember? You could get in for a gram,
stay all night – everybody, music people, movies, Wall
Street, fashion – even politics. I think like five marriages
came out of those parties, babies – really. God.

John eyes her: why this Niagara, this nostalgia?

You stayed, you then Robert – but he . . . I'da never thought
you'd, what is it, twelve years? Others, lucky a year max,
eight months, in, out, start using, unreliable – nice kids.
Remember when you first came: long hair, dirty fingers –

LETOUR
(*overlapping*)

You made me –

ANN

– never washed –

LETOUR

– khaki pants.

ANN

I should write a book some day. Did you know somebody
wanted to do my story? Ghostwrite. It was impossible, of
course – my lawyer freaked I even had the meeting. People
envy me. They think my life is so glamorous, but they
don't know. I know. *Glamorous.*
(*beat*)
It was for a while. Then came crack and fucked everything.

John wonders: the Big Goodbye? Is she acting at Tis's behest?

> LETOUR
>
> I gotta stop home a second.

> ANN
>
> Why? It's out of the way. They're expecting you.

'They're?'

> LETOUR
>
> You know I got a bad vibe about Tis.

> ANN
> (*unconvincing*)
>
> Chill. This is routine.

> LETOUR
>
> I want to get my lucky jacket.

> ANN
>
> Oh. OK.

The sedan continues south. It turns and stops in front of John's Chelsea apartment building.

John hops out and goes in.

Inside John's apartment he – a man possessed – pulls his black tweed from the closet and throws it on the futon. He rolls up his shirt, reaches under the futon, and removes the .38.

He straps the gun to his back and wraps duct tape around his chest, end to end over the .38. He tucks in his shirt, puts on the jacket, and checks the mirror to see if the gun shows: it doesn't. A pause to appreciate.

LeTour closes his diary and throws it out the window: a trifle. He slaps cologne on his cheeks – anointing; he heads toward the door.

Outside, LeTour emerges, walks quickly to the car, and plops beside Ann. The sedan drives off. Back seat:

> ANN
>
> That took long enough. What did you do, douche while you were at it?

LETOUR

Ann, you got some mouth on you.

ANN

You don't want to know where it's been.
(*sniffs him*)
Cologne?

LETOUR

For you.

ANN

Phew. It smells like that stuff they give you on airplanes.
It's no good for your skin. All chemicals.

LeTour pulls out a slip of paper and writes a name and address:
'Linda Wichel, 1012B-2 A Street, Sacramento, California.'

What's that?

LETOUR

Do me a favor.

ANN

What?

LETOUR

Don't ask why, just promise.

ANN

What is it?

LETOUR
(*testing again*)
If anything happens to me – if I should like, you know,
fucking die – write and tell her.

He extends the slip of paper.

Ann starts to speak, then stops.

It's my sister. Her husband's in San Quentin. She worries,
you know.

Ann takes the name and address.

> ANN
> (*eye contact*)

OK.

Ann, sad, looks out the window. She touches his knee.

The car pulls in front of the Pennsylvania Hotel, 34th and 7th.

> LETOUR

I thought we were going to Tis's?

> ANN

We are. He's here. He can't very well work out of his
apartment after what happened yesterday, can he?

They get out.

CUT TO:

SHOOT-OUT

*Pennsylvania lobby: a baseball-card convention is in progress. Ann
squeezes through and goes to the house phone. John follows and
scans the tacky lobby: what's up?*

> ANN
> (*on phone*)

Mathis Bruge, please.
> (*beat*)

Tis? Ann. I'm here with Tour.
> (*beat*)

OK.

She hangs up.

> LETOUR

Tis there?

> ANN

Twelve-oh-four.

*They go to the elevators, wait with chatty card collectors (Pete Rose
this, Pete Rose that).*

Twelfth floor. Ann and John step out of the elevator and look for 1204.

LeTour, a step behind, is all eyes, all ears.

Ann checks the number and rings the bell.

Thomas lets them in the standard-issue suite and locks the door.

LeTour was right: it's a set-up. Thomas and a teenage Cuban stand either side of them, waistbands conspicuously bulging. No Tis. John turns to Ann:

> LETOUR
> (*Jesus to Judas*)
>
> Ann.

Ann's confused, then furious: she had no part in the 'set-up.' In fact, she doesn't even know it's a set-up. Bursting rage, she turns on Thomas and yells:

> ANN
>
> I told you greasy fucks I don't deal with guns! I see guns, I walk! How dare you?

She slaps Thomas, pulls the 9mm from his waistband, and throws it to the carpet.

The Cuban watches bewildered, gun drawn, awaiting instructions. Now Ann's on him.

> And you, beaner, whoever the fuck you are, kiss my fat ass!

She spits on his shirt, knees him in the crotch, yanks his gun, and throws it beside the gut-clutching Cuban. She crosses the room, yelling:

> That's it! TIS! Shitball! I know you're fucking there! Let this be a lesson! You wanna deal, you gonna apologize for this!
>
> (*to LeTour*)
>
> Let's go.

Thomas and the Cuban teen retrieve their guns; Ann unlocks the door.

> THOMAS
> (*pointing gun*)

Hold it! Stop right there.

Ann turns defiantly. Tis enters from bedroom.

> TIS
> (*to Thomas*)

No!

> (*to Ann*)

Sorry about the guns. My fuck-up. I was just trying to
make a point – I apologize.

*Tis looks to Thomas and the Cuban: they lower their weapons. He
only means to threaten LeTour.*

> (*about Thomas and Cuban*)

Assholes. What a nightmare.

> (*to Ann*)

We'll make the deal tomorrow – same terms. Ann. Sorry.
Go on, leave, you're upset. I just need to talk to Tour a
second. About a police matter.

> (*to LeTour*)

Right?

> LETOUR
> (*to Ann*)

Go on.

She hesitates.

> TIS

Tour and I need to get our stories straight. Somebody's
talking to the police. The guns were for emphasis, to make
a point, dumb –

Ann gets it. Fear hits.

> ANN
> (*to Tis*)

We came together, *we're* leaving together.

(*to LeTour*)
Johnny, come with me.

She opens the door.

TIS
(*a command*)
Thomas.

Thomas fixes his gun on Ann.

(*to Ann*)
Don't be stupid. Get out. Leave.
(*to LeTour*)
I had nothing to do with Marianne – she jumped: she was
there, then she was gone.
(*nods Ann to leave*)
Nothing will happen to Tour.

Ann computes, bolts out, flees, screaming at the top of her lungs:

ANN (O.S.)
Fire! Fire! Fire!

The fire bell rings.

*Thomas, Tis, and the Cuban stare dumbfounded. LeTour reaches
behind his shirt in the confusion, yanks out the .38 with a painful
rip, turns, and fires point-blank into the Cuban's chest. BLAM!
Shirt fabric flares, flies: the Cuban falls with a blank expression.*

*Thomas, off guard, wheels and fires wildly at LeTour. John fires
back. Both are hit. Tis ducks into the bedroom. Thomas and LeTour
fire again, again – hitting, missing. A bullet hits its mark: Thomas,
frozen, grabs his blood-spurting throat and slumps to floor.*

*LeTour bleeds from the stomach and shoulder. His shirt soaks red; he
struggles to stand. Cuban and Thomas – both dead. LeTour checks
the .38: five rounds fired – one left. He staggers into the bedroom,
finds Tis frantically searching an open suitcase. Off-screen voices
under the fire bell.*

TIS
(*desperate*)
I didn't –

LeTour steps to Tis, aims, and shoots him barrel to forehead. Exit debris hits the wall. He is dead.

Off-screen screams of guests are countered by commands from hotel security: 'Get down!' 'Get back!' Fire horns and sirens reverb from the street.

LeTour, losing consciousness, sits bedside. The gun slips from his hand.

Deflating, he drifts back-first to the bedspread. Blood spreads. His eyes are open.

Police voices approach.

FADE OUT.

EVERY GRAIN OF SAND

Prison waiting area. Ann, wearing a wool suit, waits among black/Hispanic friends and relatives. The first scene without LeTour: she sits quietly. A corrections officer instructs the visitors to proceed.

Ann walks through a concrete corridor and finds the visiting area.

LeTour, in prison fatigues, sits at a table. He sees her and smiles.

Ann sits down. This is not her first visit.

LETOUR
Hello.

ANN
Hi.

She checks watch.

LETOUR
Twenty minutes. You look terrific.

ANN

I look respectable. Any news?

LETOUR

Sentencing's in ten days – supposed to be. Because of the
extenuating circumstances – our cooperation – they say it
won't be more than five years – maybe seven. With time
served, good behavior, parole, I could be out in two years
– maybe. I hope.

ANN

It feels like for ever.

LETOUR

It's not so bad. It's a relief in a way – at least so far. I've
been writing, reading.

ANN

I love your letters.

Pause.

LETOUR

How's business?

ANN

Robert quit. He went back to dealing. I think he thought
it would be less work, more money. It's lucky in a way I
got mixed up in it – now I have to see this thing through.
So it's cosmetics after all.

LETOUR
(affectionate)

I miss you.

ANN

Me too.

LETOUR

Did we ever fuck?

ANN

What do you mean?

LETOUR

You know, make love.

ANN
(*thinks*)

There was that party when everybody was so stoned, but –
oh yeah, that night you came over and crashed and we
slept together.

LETOUR

We were naked, but did we –?

ANN

You had a hard-on . . .

LETOUR

I didn't –

ANN

You tried . . .

LETOUR

I was thinking about it and I realized we never really did.
It's one of the things I think about. It's one of the things I
look forward to. I've been looking forward.

ANN

Me too.

LETOUR
(*touches her hand*)

Something can be right in front of you and you can't see
it.

ANN
(*kisses his hand*)

Strange how things work.

The tableau fades.